YOUR WINE QUESTIONS ANSWERED
Published by © Citizen Press Ltd. London, 2016
ISBN 978-0-9551363-4-4
© Jerry Lockspeiser, 2016

A CIP record for this book is available from the British Library
Citizen Press is an Imprint of Gudrun Publishing
www.citizen-press.co.uk

Printed in India

Contents

Foreword

by Amanda Redman, actress and wine drinker.

When I was first asked to write a foreword to "Your Wine Questions Answered" I accepted with more than a little trepidation. I know absolutely nothing about wine even though it is consumed by the barrel full at our house. However it was for a good cause, so in I plunged. After all, as someone wiser than I noted, the book is actually for ignoramuses such as myself – which indeed was the point of asking me!

Now, I know what I like in wine and indeed what I don't, but have no idea why I've made these preferences. This wonderful little book has made things so much clearer for me.

It is incredibly easy to read and never once patronises or makes one feel like the aforesaid ignoramus. It is completely devoid of the snobbery usually associated with wine buffs and lays out the facts in simple terms. Even I can remember the Four Handles (or most basic things to take into consideration) when choosing wine. Country, Grape, Region or Brand.

I especially like "In One Gulp" at the end of each chapter which sums up the topic in a few lines.

The underlying message seems to be that taste is personal and we should never feel embarrassed or intimidated when ordering what we like. The fact that screw tops are ok is an added bonus.

Indeed my favourite quote when describing the differences in production of sparkling wines uses terms to which I can completely relate by likening them to clothes' designers. Champagne is Stella McCartney, Cava is Cos and Prosecco is Top Shop.

Personally I adore Stella McCartney but then again I'm also extremely partial to Top Shop.

Amanda Redman, London

o expensive wines are better? Is RED WINE GO FOR HEALTH? HOULD I TRUST THE MED N WINE BOTTLES? Why do HAT IS A CORKED professio INE? wine tasters slur chew wine? hat IS THE DIFFERENCE BETWEEN N MPA NE & do they CAV some IS es have WIN berrys? GOOD IT HEA UE?

What this book is for and how to use it

Do you find wine confusing? Is buying it a shot in the dark?

The majority of us drink wine at some time. The money we spend on it puts billions of pounds into the tills of shops and restaurants. But most of us understand little about what we are buying.

The purpose of this book is to change that.

Over the years I have met thousands of wine drinkers from every walk of life, from nurses to plumbers, from lawyers to musicians. Many of them, after some initial awkwardness, have opened up and told me what they really wanted to know. This book is the answer to their questions.

You will discover:

- How to interpret the label and choose with greater confidence

- The essential differences between wines and why they don't all taste the same

- The relationship between price, quality and value

- How to drink with greater knowledge and freedom – including knowing when it's fine to choose red wine with fish

You'll find out why your eyes are more important than your tongue, why wine is like rugby, how most people prefer cheap to expensive wine, why Brad Pitt and Angelina Jolie's wine is hard to understand and a whole lot more.

There are twenty five chapters between two and eight pages long. Some are mainly factual, answering questions such as which wines have the fewest calories and what it means when a wine is 'corked'. Others – such as whether red wine is good for health and if it matters what kind of glass you drink out of – are open to different interpretations and opinions.

Each chapter is self-contained and can be read independently of the others. If you have a burning desire to know about a particular question do go there first. However the order is deliberate. The early chapters about how to read the bottle and understand the wine inside serve as a foundation for the questions about how to choose, buy, keep and drink the stuff.

The questions are explored and answered in less time than it takes to drink a small glass. At the end of each chapter, IN ONE GULP gives the nub of the answer in the time it takes to swallow a mouthful.

Wine can feel as complex as nuclear physics and as scary as sky diving. It doesn't need to be. It's just a bottle of fermented grapes. Wine can be understandable. This book will show you how.

What is Cabernet Sauvignon ?

Twenty-six million of us drink wine regularly in the UK. We buy around 1.7 billion bottles every year and spend £12 billion. We drink wine more often than either beer or spirits. Most of us buy wine in supermarkets, giving them a huge 75% share of the market. The average shopper spends more on wine in a supermarket than any other category, beating frozen food in second place and fresh meat in third.

But despite the huge financial outlay most of us are shooting blind.

One of the country's biggest wine suppliers wanted to find out what wine drinkers know about the wines they buy. They talked to many thousands of people, younger and older, men and women, experienced drinkers and those new to wine. Among their questions were some about the words on the bottle, such as what is Cabernet Sauvignon? Rioja? Chenin Blanc?

Of those questioned 42% knew that Chenin Blanc was a grape variety used to make white wines. Looked at the other way round, this means more than half had no idea what the word meant when they saw it on a label. Only 28%, just over a quarter, correctly identified Rioja as a region. Cabernet Sauvignon split down the middle with 50% knowing it's a type of grape, the others not. Of the thirteen questions only 5% of respondents got more than half right. That means a whopping 95% were wrong more often than they were right.

Many people find buying wine difficult. This is not because they are stupid. The meaning of the words is not clear, the language is complex and the flavour is a mystery. It is hardly surprising that confusion and anxiety are common. We would probably buy more, with greater enjoyment of doing so, if the people who sell wine made it easier to understand.

But it used to be a whole lot worse.

Until about 25 years ago, wines from Australia, New Zealand, Chile and South Africa were nowhere to be seen. France, Italy and Germany dominated the UK market. These countries bamboozled us with incomprehensible names that didn't sound like wine at all. Sarget de Gruaud Larose – isn't that an uncomfortable type of back pain? Morellinodi Scansano Poggioargentiera

– that'll be the dangerous new bacteria from Italy. Spätburgunder Weis- sherbst Spätlese – sounds more like a serious psychological illness than something nice to sip over dinner.

However the 'Old World' European countries of France, Italy and Spain did have method in their madness. Historically, the name on the label was the property where the vineyards were located and the grapes were processed into wine. Château this or Domaine that in France, Bodega something in Spain, Tenuta something else in Italy- all these refer to the property the wine comes from. This was coupled with the name of the region to give a broader statement of identity and so a suggestion of taste, quality and reputation. Château Vieux-Georget in Bordeaux, Bodegas Bagordi in Rioja or Tenuta San Vito in Chianti are examples.

This way of communicating often didn't state what type of grapes the wine was made from, or what it tasted like. Some producers didn't bother with back labels, believing that the name of their property and the prestige of the region were sufficient to win customers over. Then the Europeans got their comeuppance.

Towards the end of the 1980s, 'New World' wines from Australia, New Zealand and California began to appear. At first no more than a dribble, they grew into a swiftly flowing river before becoming a veritable tsunami, and now they are everywhere.

New World wines took root because they gave us what we craved. While the European wines were designed to go with food and were often sharp and harsh to drink, these were a softer, fruitier style and easy to drink at any time. Where the European wines were inconsistent in quality from one bottle to the next, the New World wines always tasted the same. And last but not least, the words were in English. We may not have known much about Jacobs Creek or the weirdly named Wolf Blass, but at least we could pronounce them.

The New World countries' master stroke was to flip the European tradition of labelling on its head. Instead of focusing on the property and region, their labels announced the wine by brand and grape variety. With grape varieties as the compass we had a sporting chance of navigating the shelves.

Australian brands like Jacob's Creek and Peter Lehmann introduced us to the idea of matching taste to grape variety - especially Chardonnay for white wines and Shiraz for red. New Zealand wineries championed Sauvignon Blanc, the Chileans sold bucket-loads of wines made from Cabernet Sauvignon, and before long our shelves were bursting with a host of different grape varieties.

At first the Europeans scoffed at these upstarts, but when the New World 'varietally labelled' wines boomed in popularity they jumped ship. Today many European producers also use grape varieties to identify their wines.

USING GRAPE VARIETY AS THE STARTING POINT FOR CHOOSING A WINE

The grape varieties most commonly seen on labels are Chardonnay and Sauvignon Blanc for white wines and Cabernet Sauvignon and Merlot for reds. These four are planted all over the world. And where they are planted makes a big difference to what they taste like.

If you order a glass of Sauvignon Blanc without knowing which country it comes from you could be in for a shock. Sauvignon Blanc from New Zealand and Sauvignon Blanc from France have very different tastes. The taste may also vary significantly between different regions within the same country, such as Sauvignon Blanc from the north and south of France.

To find a wine you like, nothing beats having a sip. Where this isn't possible, look for the key determinants of taste: country, grape, region and brand. The more you can remember the taste of these, especially in combination with each other, the greater your chance of choosing something you will like.

FREQUENTLY SEEN GRAPE VARIETIES

White wines: Sauvignon Blanc, Chardonnay, Pinot Grigio, Chenin Blanc, Semillon

Red wines: Merlot, Shiraz, Cabernet Sauvignon, Pinot Noir, Tempranillo, Malbec, Grenache (also known as Garnacha)

FREQUENTLY SEEN REGIONS

France: Bordeaux, Burgundy, Cotes du Rhône, Chablis, Sancerre

Spain: Rioja

Italy: Chianti, Soave

Wines from these well-known European regions often only state the grape variety on the back label because they do not want, or are not permitted, to put it on the front. New World wines also come from specific regions but usually focus instead on the grape and country.

To identify wine styles that you like start with one of the four 'handles' (country, grape, region or brand) as the anchor, then work your way through the others in combination. For example, if you like a Sauvignon Blanc, identify the country it came from. Then try other Sauvignon Blancs from the same country and note which regions or brands you prefer. Or try Sauvignon Blanc wines from different countries, noting which style you like most. You will soon narrow and define your preference.

The problem is to remember. How many times have you loved a wine but forgotten what it was and not been able to find it again? When you drink something you really like, take a photo of the label.

IN ONE GULP

Cabernet Sauvignon is one of the world's major grape varieties and is used to produce wines in many countries. Grape varieties are shown on wine labels to indicate the style and flavour of the wine. It's one of the four main indicators of what a particular wine might taste like, along with the name of the region where the wine was produced, the country and the brand name. Out of these, grape variety and country are the most important, and their combination is the foundation of taste.

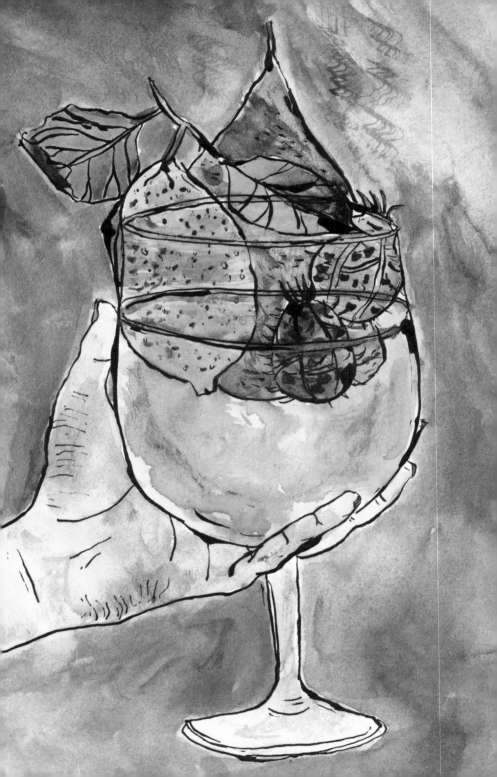

Why do they say
some wines have

'A hint of
gooseberries' ?

Most of us have no idea what a wine will taste like before we buy it for the first time. Wine producers and retailers use descriptions of flavours they think we are familiar with to give us a clue. This is hard to do well. When it is done badly, it may as well be written in Latin.

In June 2013, highly regarded wine merchants Berry Bros & Rudd announced their importation of a rather special rosé. It came from Château Miraval in the Provence region of southern France, a wine estate owned by Brad Pitt and Angelina Jolie.

The wine was made under the expert control of renowned wine maker Marc Perrin from organically grown grapes. Brangelina were involved in the wine's creation and put their names on the back label. It cost £18.95 a bottle.

So what did it taste like?

Here is how Berry Bros described the wine:

"The transparent Ruinart-style bottle allows the evanescent almost luminous colours to tease a gentle pink. The blend is equally shared by Cinsault, Grenache, Syrah and Rolle (aka Vermentino), with the Syrah partially macerated on its skin by the saignée method.

Aromatics of forest floor and wild strawberry with hints of herb, cede to an impressive palate, reassuringly yet deceptively powerful. Flinty, citric notes underwrite a classic red fruit core, all in a subtle minor key but with a resonant, eloquent finish. Ideal to match fruits de mer or salade niçoise."

Come again?

Berry Bros are a great old school wine merchant, and they no doubt have some pretty knowledgeable customers, but this kind of description is incomprehensible to 99% of wine drinkers. Unfortunately Berrys are by no means the only ones to get it wrong.

Winegrowers of Ara in New Zealand make a Sauvignon Blanc called Comosite. Great drink, terrible description on the back label:

"Composite Sauvignon Blanc is a contemporary expression of terroir from wine growers of Ara. Selected lots meld into intense, ripe stone-and-grapefruit characters, concentrated with generous mouthfeel and a long clean finish."

And from the back label of a South African wine called The Wild Olive Old Vines Chenin Blanc, this is not much better:

"A beautifully balanced Chenin Blanc with notes of gooseberry and apple. The finish is long with an elegant minerality."

Supermarkets and major brands take a more down-to-earth approach with the language on their back labels, but their efforts to communicate the taste can also go awry.

The problem with 'tastes of this' and 'smells of that' – what wine buffs call 'on the palate' and 'on the nose' – is that we each taste and smell differently. If you stick your nose into a glass of Australian Chardonnay and inhale deeply, you may find a smell that reminds you of, say, apricots. With the exact same glass of wine another person may smell something else – for example, butter. If the back label says it has a smell of apricots, which you like the sound of, but on pouring a glass it smells to you of butter, which you want on your toast but not in your wine, you won't be too pleased.

A few wines do have smells (aromas) that just about everyone identifies in the same way. A lot of people think that many Sauvignon Blanc wines from New Zealand have a smell of gooseberries. But sure fire winners like this are rare.

As one person's apricot is another person's butter, such detailed descriptions often don't help to identify a taste you will like. Coffee packets tell us whether it's strong or mild, dark or light, good for breakfast or dinner.

The wine equivalent is to describe it as dry or sweet, fruity or crisp, light or strong. Describing wine in these more understandable terms is a better starting point.

The popular White Zinfandel (actually rosé) from California in brands such as Blossom Hill, Gallo and Echo Falls is a good example for these simpler descriptive terms. It's a light, fruity style of wine. Pinot Grigio from Italy has become the 'go to' white wine for many people because of its light, soft, easy drinking flavour.

Once you have identified a general style that you like – dry or sweet, fruity or crisp, light or strong – and found a wine that corresponds to that, for example Californian White Zinfandel or Italian Pinot Grigio, make a mental note of the smells or flavours you associate with it. It can be anything at all, from blackberries to seaweed, lemons to chocolate, Muller Lite Strawberry Yoghurt to petrol. Or it might simply be light and fresh, or heavy and alcoholic. Whatever comes to you is your reference. Never mind what anyone else says.

Next time you find the same characteristics in a different wine, check the label to see if they have anything in common – for example, same grape, region or country. In this way you can gradually build up a memory of which wines have which flavours for you. And that means being able to choose with greater success.

IN ONE GULP

Tastes and smells can be extremely subjective and wine experts are often unhelpfully obscure in their descriptions. But a reference to a smell or taste we're already familiar with can be helpful in describing a wine. Of course there are no gooseberries in a Sauvignon Blanc but the gooseberry-like taste is a handy reference point.

What does the year on the label mean?

It's the year in which the grapes used to make the wine were picked.

Once harvested, grapes are taken as quickly as possible to the winery for processing. Fresh grapes retain natural fruit flavours. Winemaking starts within hours of the grapes being picked, and although it may take many months to complete, once it's underway the year of the wine is confirmed.

In the English-speaking world the wine harvest is called the vintage. In Spain it's the vendimia or cosecha, in France the millesime and in Italy the vendemmia. It's an oddity that vintage cars and vintage clothes are old, but vintage wine could have been made yesterday. It simply means a wine whose harvest date has been identified.

The harvest date matters because of variation in the quality of grapes, and hence of the wine, in different years. But thanks to the Australians, today's wines are much more consistent from year to year than they used to be.

In the past, northern hemisphere European wines – especially French, Italian, Spanish and German – were pretty much all that was available on our shelves. The traditional European approach to winemaking was fairly hands-off, leaving the quality of the grapes and the wine to the power of sun, rain and God. As the climate fluctuated from year to year, so did the quality of the wine. All too often a nice tasting vintage of Chianti, Côtes du Rhône or Rioja was followed by a disappointing one twelve months later.

In contrast, southern hemisphere countries like Australia, New Zealand, Chile and South Africa had less natural climate variation. They were also uninhibited by the European traditions of grape-growing and winemaking. From the 1980s onwards, Australia, New Zealand and California produced a new type of wine maker with a completely different approach.

The young pretenders from the other side of the world didn't wait to see what nature provided. They decided in advance what flavour they wanted in the wine, and introduced new vineyard techniques and winery processes to achieve it. And they aimed to make it taste that way every year.

For them the process was both a technical and commercial challenge. Grapes were a fruit in a field to be turned into an alcoholic drink that people would enjoy. Unlike the Europeans, they treated wine as a food product and made their wineries and equipment spotlessly clean. And they worked 24/7 to ensure the wine turned out just as they wanted it.

Having mastered this approach at home, they took their ideas to Europe. The response of a proud Frenchman being told how to process his grapes by a young backpacker from Adelaide surely doesn't need describing. But after much slamming of doors, gnashing of teeth and heels dug firmly into the ground, many European wine producers adopted the Australian principles. Nature still makes the harvest in Europe more fickle than down under, but the way of dealing with it has been upgraded enormously. It's as though the Europeans have moved from black and white terrestrial TV to the full Sky HD package. As a result their wines are a lot more consistent from year to year than they used to be.

This is all good news. It means that the days when the 2005 Rioja was delicious but the 2006 was pretty rough have largely disappeared. The vintage is now often written in tiny letters on the label, reflecting its reduced importance to the taste.

The new techniques greatly reduce the variation in wine quality from year to year, but they cannot eliminate it altogether. Most countries allow 15% of wine from a different year to be added, thus ironing out the differences, while still putting the main vintage on the label.

Some wines do not have a vintage printed on the label. This means the wine could be a blend of several different years, and allows the blender greater flexibility in the search for a constant style. Unsurprisingly such wines are called 'non-vintage'.

If you drink white or rosé wines you should pay attention to the year on the label. With a few exceptions everyday white and rosé wines are at their best when they are young. The fresh fruit character that makes them so attractive fades with age. So make sure the year on the bottle is no more than two years ago. Red wines generally keep their quality for longer – and some are deliberately made to be drunk when they are older – but once they are in the shops they are better drunk than kept.

WHEN VINTAGE MEANS MONEY

The vintage concept really comes into its own in Bordeaux in France. Not the normal wines from Bordeaux, but the great and expensive wines that change hands for hundreds or thousands of pounds – names like Mouton-Rothschild, Margaux, Lafite and Petrus.

These wines exist in a parallel universe with its own markets. In much the same way that people buy an apartment 'off the plan', investors purchase wines of top-notch Châteaux soon after they are made, and many years before they are bottled or ready to drink. Only available in limited quantities investors buy early, hoping that the price will rise and they will make a hefty profit by reselling them later. They may be bought and sold many times before they are eventually, if ever, drunk. But as with property, 'fine wine' prices may not rise as expected and fingers can get burnt.

These wines are made from grapes of a single vintage and the quality each year is keenly followed. A high-quality harvest means the potential for sky-high prices in future, as both the wine and investment mature.

The opinions of a few significant commentators about the quality of the vintage are the key in determining demand for the wines and the price the Châteaux charge. The man whose opinion has counted more than any other over the last 30 years is American wine critic Robert Parker. Parker is the king-maker. A high score from him almost guarantees a high price and strong demand.

Back in the real world, wine enthusiasts without such deep pockets enjoy discovering a small producer they like and buying bottles from different vintages. If 'getting into wine' appeals to you, then comparing the subtle shifts in style from one year to another can be fun. It's like a music-lover following the new songs from a favourite band.

The significance of the year depends on what you are looking for in a wine. For everyday drinkers, eradicating the difference between vintages is the aim. For wine enthusiasts looking for interest, and investors looking for profit, identifying the difference between them is what counts.

IN ONE GULP

The vintage is the year in which the grapes used to make the wine were picked. For everyday wines it's not as important as a guide to quality now that new techniques have made wine more consistent from year to year, though for more expensive and specialist wines it still is.

What is the difference between Champagne and Cava?

Understanding things about wine can start in the most unlikely places. Take my journey with Champagne on a boat down the Yangtze River in China.

I was standing on the deck marvelling at the view when a waitress approached holding a tray of fluted plastic glasses.

"Would you like a glass of Champagne?" she asked. At that moment I couldn't have thought of anything more perfect. The wine was cold enough, but didn't taste very fresh. It seemed to be one of the sweeter styles, with a lighter flavour than I remembered. Then I began to think that free Champagne on a big tourist boat in the middle of the Yangtze wasn't very likely. Two gulps later I was pretty sure that I wasn't drinking real Champagne.

I asked the waitress if I could see the bottle. It wasn't Champagne. Nor was it Cava, Prosecco or any other kind of sparkling wine made from grapes. It was a brand of Perry, a sparkling wine look-a-like drink made from pears that came in a large bottle with a plastic cork. But it was fizzy and cold and was served in a Champagne-style glass. To the crew of the boat it was Champagne. And to the other holiday-makers happily downing glass after glass it was Champagne too. It made me think, so what if it's not real Champagne? What's in a name? Who cares so long as people enjoy it?

The Champagne producers care. They care desperately. Champagne is a region in eastern France where sparkling wines are made. The people there insist that only their sparkling wines have the right to use the name Champagne. They have spent an enormous amount of time and money defending their exclusive use of the name. After many legal battles around the world, they have pretty much won the war. Other sparkling wines made in Europe, Australia, Chile and many other countries can't be called Champagne.

The Champagne producers know that this word is their passport to high prices and the world of luxury goods. Some other wines are very expensive, but they still feel like wines. Champagne has set itself apart. It is the embodiment of luxury and celebration.

Cava is not Champagne. It is a sparkling wine produced in Spain which uses the same techniques but different grapes.

There are different ways of producing fizz in sparkling wines. The 'Champagne' method creates the fizz individually in each bottle. This is the most expensive way to fizz wine and produces the best quality bubbles. Cava is also made this way, so can claim to be Champagne's less affluent neighbour.

The two key differences between Champagne and Cava are the flavour, which comes from the different kinds of grapes used, and the price.

The higher price is partly due to higher production costs. Champagne grapes cost more than Cava grapes, and land, labour and other factors are more expensive in Champagne. Cava must be kept (aged) for at least nine months after it has been produced before it is allowed to be sold. Champagne must be aged for a minimum of fifteen months, so it costs more to finance.

But these higher costs do not explain all of the price difference. The rest is down to the luxury image, and the well-controlled balance between the amount produced and the world-wide demand. Champagne prices are high because they can be.

Well-known Champagne brands like Moët & Chandon, Lanson or Mumm sell for between three and five times the price of the biggest Cava brands Freixenet and Cordoníu. Super-expensive deluxe Champagne brands such as Dom Perignon and Louis Roederer Cristal have developed this opportunity to the full and command sky-high prices.

At the opposite end of the spectrum are the supermarket own-label Champagnes. Their cheaper price does not necessarily mean they taste worse than branded rivals such as Moët, Lanson and the others. Several have beaten the big brands in professional tasting competitions. They are cheaper because the supermarkets buy big quantities, sell them at lower profit margins, and don't have brand marketing budgets to pay for. The comparison between supermarket Champagnes and the big brands is similar to that between high street clothes and designer labels.

Cava is not the only cheaper sparkling wine made in the same way as Champagne. The French wines called 'Crémant de' somewhere – Crémant de Bourgogne (Burgundy) and Crémant d'Alsace for example – are made this way, as are many sparkling wines from other countries.

Because they are not allowed to use the word Champagne, you will often see 'Bottle fermented' or 'Traditional method' on the label. This is code for saying "I am made in the same way as Champagne, so I am great quality too."

On the other hand, many sparkling wines use a cheaper system of getting the fizz into the bottle. The most common is to ferment the wine a second time in a huge tank, trapping the bubbles produced by the fermentation, and piping the wine into each bottle. Italian Prosecco and most of the Australian sparklers are made this way. Their fizz is created in a more industrial way but they are perfectly good drinks.

So here's a question. If you have a glass of sparkling wine, can you tell which method of producing the bubbles was used? Do you care? If you don't see the bottle can you tell if you are drinking Champagne, Cava or Prosecco?

The bubbles take focus away from the difference in taste, which starts with the kind of grapes the wines are made from. Champagne may be made from any of Chardonnay, Pinot Noir and Pinot Meunier. Prosecco is principally made from a grape called Glera. Cava is made from Macabeu, Parellada and Xarell-lo. Each of these grapes has different flavours, just as Braeburn, Royal Gala, Cox and Granny Smith apples taste different to each other. Many factors influence the taste, but the type of grape is where it all starts. The grapes used in Champagne are considered the best.

Every producer makes their wine differently, so making broad comments about the typical flavour of any type is asking for trouble. But here goes: Cava is usually drier and less fruity than similar-priced Prosecco, which is softer and less tart. Champagne is richer and crisper than both.

Whether to buy Champagne or sparkling wine comes down to two equally important questions. Do you like the taste? And do you want to make a statement?

THE TASTE

It sounds crazy, but what we see or hear affects our taste as much as what we put in our mouth. Test it out. Next time you have friends round, ask them if they would like a glass of Champagne but give them a glass of Cava. Don't let them see the bottle. How many of them say anything other than how nice the Champagne is?

Try taking this a step further by involving your friends in a sociable game that is sure to get them talking. Buy a bottle each of Champagne, Prosecco, Cava and any other sparkling wine, such as an Australian or one of the Crémants from France. Number them from one to four and put them in the fridge to chill.

Next, mark four champagne flute glasses in the same way (post-it note or removable-ink pen). When the wine is cold, pour some from each numbered bottle into the matching glass. Give each guest a piece of paper and pen. Ask them to take a sip of each of the four glasses and write down the number of the one they like most. It's important you tell them to keep their opinions to themselves. People shouting out with delight or looking as if they have been poisoned will influence the others.

When everyone has written down the number of the wine they liked most, collect the pieces of paper and rank the results.

Before declaring the winner, tell your friends what they have been drink-ing – a Prosecco, a Champagne and so on – but not which wine was which number. Then announce the number that got the most votes and ask them to guess which type of wine it is, before revealing the bottle to them. Continue with the second most popular number through all four wines.

It is unlikely that everyone will pick the Champagne as their favourite even though it will be the most expensive. They are more likely to choose based on their taste preference for sweet, fruity, crisp and so on.

MAKING A STATEMENT

Give someone a bottle of Cava for their birthday and it's a gift of a bottle of wine. Give someone a bottle of Champagne and it's a statement of how much you value them. Champagne says 'special'. It doesn't say "I bought this because I think it's a nicer taste than Cava".

A WORD OF WARNING

There are different styles within the range of Champagne and other sparkling wines, just as there are different styles within chocolate. They come in dry, medium and sweeter versions. The words used to describe them are very confusing.

'Brut' means dry, 'Extra Dry' is sweeter than Brut, 'Medium Dry' is sweeter again - and much sweeter than the words suggest. Sparkling wines are sweeter than the equivalent still wines. For example, Brut (dry) Champagne is sweeter than dry still wine. Brut is the most widely sold style and it's wise to stick with this unless you like medium wines, in which case go for Extra Dry, or sweet wines, in which case go for Medium Dry.

IN ONE GULP

Champagne is only produced in the Champagne region of France. Cava is a sparkling wine produced in Spain. They use the same method of creating the fizz but different grapes. For Prosecco both the method of creating the fizz and the grapes are different. In production terms Champagne is Stella McCartney, Cava is Cos and Prosecco is Top Shop. But only you can decide how to rank them for taste.

Why does French Chardonnay taste different to Australian Chardonnay?

Wine is like rugby.

The French and Australian rugby teams play the same game but they don't play it in the same way. Their approach has developed in different climates over considerable time. They have different traditions, cultures and training regimes. As a result their tactics and style of play are different.

It's the same for their wines.

A wine tastes as it does because of a combination of natural and human factors. Soil is not just dirt. It contains different elements that affect the grapes grown on the vines. The climate – especially the amount of sun and rain – affects how the vines grow. The way the plants are cared for in the vineyard impacts the quality of the grapes. And the processes used to turn the grapes into wine dramatically affect the flavours in the bottle.

Even when the grape variety is the same, such as Chardonnay, these four areas lead to big differences in the taste of the wine.

Imagine that French and Australian producers both made wines from Chardonnay grapes and used identical methods in the vineyard and the winemaking. Their wines would still taste different becauseof the natural factors. The soil, sunlight, water and temperature create the base for the flavour.

In reality the French and Australians do not use identical practices. Instead they adapt to their individual circumstances and to the style of wine they want to create in the bottles we buy.

The extra sun in Australia generally makes their grapes and their wines more of everything – more alcoholic, more fully-flavoured, riper and fruitier. The relatively cooler French climate leans the other way. The wines taste crisper and less alcoholic, with flavours that are less fruity and 'in your face'.

The overriding importance of the climate is reflected in the choice on the shelves. We know New Zealand for its Sauvignon Blanc white wines because their cool climate is perfect for producing this variety. But it's not so good for producing the powerfully flavoured red wines we tend to like, which is why we don't see so many New Zealand reds. Those that do make it over here are mostly made from Pinot Noir grapes, a red grape suited to their cooler climate that produces less muscular wines.

In the days when wines from Eastern Europe were cheap and popular, Hungarian wines were everywhere. 80% were white. Like New Zealand, their climate is not hot enough for the red grapes to ripen sufficiently and produce the rich fruity style we like to drink. Bulgaria, further south and hotter than Hungary, is the opposite, and had much greater success with reds than whites.

Perhaps the red wine that shows the overriding importance of the climate most clearly is Cabernet Sauvignon. This grape variety needs a warm climate to ripen and become really juicy, like succulent strawberries or blackberries. Cabernets from Australia or Bulgaria have this style. But grown in cooler climates with less sunshine, the grapes do not ripen as much and the flavour is tart, like redcurrants or under-ripe cherries.

The taste of a wine begins with nature but continues with the people who make it. Just as a potter moulds a piece of clay into a specific style of pot, so a winemaker processes grapes to achieve a specific style of wine. But the choices they make do not exist in a vacuum. They reflect and respond to the culture they are working in.

So it's not surprising that a country's wines share many characteristics with its people. National stereotypes are a sweeping generalisation not to be taken too seriously. But there is no smoke without fire. Below are stereo-types of the people from four well-known wine producing countries. See if you recognise them. The answers follow immediately after.

Upfront, outgoing, obvious, self-confident (Clearly not the French)

Stylish, romantic, disorganised, cultured (Not the Germans or English)

Passionate, colourful, expressive, relaxed (Not the New Zealanders)

Elegant, sophisticated, arrogant, aloof (Not the Australians)

They are, in order:

the Australians, Italians, Spanish and French.

That was the people – but it's also the wines. If you want straightforward, bold up-front flavours, go for Australia. If you are looking for elegance and sophistication, stay in France. Italy offers a patchwork of stylish tastes, while Spain is passionate and expressive.

The similarities don't stop there. German wines are well–planned and carefully defined. Argentina brings more warmth and riotous sexy flair than its studious and better organised neighbour Chile. New Zealand delivers consistently reliable high quality. Wherever you look, wines are like the people who made them.

This means it is never wise to have a closed mind about a particular grape variety. "I don't like Chardonnay", or whatever, underestimates how varied the taste of a grape can be from one country to another. "I don't like Australian Chardonnay but I do like Italian Chardonnay" shows an appreciation of the differences, and makes more sense.

But things are on the move. The climate required to produce good wine grapes is a fragile and changing one. Global warming is affecting the way grapes develop in some countries. Potential temperature increases of up to four degrees later this century would radically change the world wine map, making some countries too hot and dry to produce grapes while bringing others into cultivation. Australia, already subject to water shortages, could be burnt out, while England, already striding ahead in the production of sparkling wine, may benefit. Wine drinkers in 2100 will have a very different choice from the one we have today.

IN ONE GULP

Wines made from the same grape taste different because of where and how they are made. The primary difference comes from the climate and land. The second comes from different ways of turning the grapes into wine. A grape variety is like a musical instrument, the result depends on who's playing the tune.

How is Rosé made ?

Rosé comes in many guises. It can be dry or sweet, barely pink or almost red, light or strongly flavoured, still or sparkling. It can be made from many different grape varieties and in every country. Once exclusively a summer drink, its popularity has grown enormously in the last 10 years and it now accounts for around 12% of wine sales in the UK. Tasting ripe, succulent, fruity and fresh, rosé is 'happy wine'.

So how is this bundle of fun made? There are white grapes and red grapes, but there aren't any rosé grapes. Here's what happens with wine and its colour.

The juice of most grapes is colourless. Once the grapes are crushed and the juice released, the winemaker has a choice – take it away immediately, or leave it in contact with the skins to absorb their colour.

White wines are mostly made from grapes with green skins. As soon as the grapes are crushed the juice is taken away from them, so it stays a whitish colour, often with a greenish tinge.

Rosé and red wines are made from grapes with black skins. In fact, they have a red or blue hue, but are called black because it's the opposite of white (even though most white wine skins are green!). The juice is left in contact with the skins to take on the colour and flavour. The greater the contact time, the darker the colour of the wine. Light rosés, often described as having an onion-skin colour, have had only a few hours' skin contact, while deeper coloured rosés – such as those from Chile or Argentina – have several days. The popular White Zinfandel or Blush from California is somewhere in the middle.

So rosé is a red wine that got stopped in its tracks. The juice is whisked away from the dark grape skins and processed alone like a white wine. As a result it tastes more like a white, with the fruitiness of the grape juice the dominant flavour. In contrast full-blown red wines left in contact with grape skins, stalks and pips, pick up harsher flavours from them.

It can be hard to identify rosé from white if you don't see what you are drinking. Blind fold your guests and hand them a glass of wine. Ask them to say what colour it is by tasting. Just about everyone will identify red wine – although some very ripe, juicy reds from Australia or California are less obvious – but rosé and white can be confused.

Rosé can also be made by adding a touch of red to a white wine. This is done in Champagne but not many other places, legally at least. Many winemakers pour scorn on such 'bastard' wines. The more commercially minded craftily blend the two together when their stocks of properly made 'skin contact' rosé are running low. As long as people like the taste, does it really matter? Try it yourself at home.

Eight things to remember about rosé:

- Always drink it cold

- Always drink it young and fresh. Check the year on the bottle and make sure it is the year you are in or the one before, but not older. You want a bright, youthful, vibrant pink colour, not orange or brown

- Check out the dry/sweetness information on the bottle. As a general rule, the popular Californian White Zinfandel is pretty sweet, European (especially French) rosés are often dry, and Australian, South African, Chilean and Argentinean are in between. But you need to check

- The darker the colour the stronger the flavour

- Rosé is a crowd pleaser. In a group where some like red and others white, a fruity European or South American rosé will win all hearts. It's versatile and a great BBQ wine

- You have permission to drink it all year round, not only in the summer

- You have permission to mix it with fruits and other drinks to make long cocktails

- Rosé is a great drink every bit as worthy as red or white

IN ONE GULP

Rosé starts life being made like red wine, but is taken away from the crushed grape skins before they give it too much colour. It is then made like a white wine and so tastes closer to white than red.

What is a corked wine?

I don't ever recall buying a faulty packet of biscuits, jar of marmalade or box of cereal. Rotting fruit and wilting vegetables are rare nowadays, and cheese, yoghurt and fish are always fresh. But as many as one in every 15 bottles of wine may be ruined. There are several things that can make a wine taste off, but a bad cork is enemy number one.

This is not about a few cork crumbs in the wine. A crumbly cork is annoying but unless it has fallen apart enough to let the air into the bottle it won't change the taste. Good corks become bad corks when they are infected with trichloroanisole or TCA for short, a harmless but miserable chemical that passes a mouldy flavour into the wine. A wine whose flavour is spoilt by TCA is said to be 'corked'.

TCA-affected wines should be returned to the shop or restaurant. No-one would hesitate to return a mobile phone that didn't receive calls or a kettle whose handle fell off. Wine should be no different. If only it were so simple.

La Grenouille was a traditional style French restaurant in Leeds. It seemed the perfect place to entertain my friends Andy and Carol Masters on their annual visit to the UK. Andy is a first class New Zealand winemaker and it was his 40th birthday.

At the end of a good meal with three different and delicious bottles of Sauvignon Blanc, we decided to finish the evening in style with Dom Perignon Rosé Champagne. DP is the Rolls Royce of Champagnes, one of the most highly regarded bottles of bubbly on the market and with a price to match.

As soon as we had taken a sip we knew something was wrong. It had the dank, mouldy smell and taste that come from a TCA-infected cork. It still tasted of wine, but the normally delicious fruity flavour was missing.

We called the waiter back to hear our bad news and requested a replacement bottle. He frowned in disbelief that anyone might reject Dom Perignon. I explained that we worked in the wine business, Andy was an internationally acclaimed winemaker, we had drunk three other bottles of wine all of which tasted fine, but this was corked and we wanted him to change it.

After 10 minutes of arguing the waiter agreed to take the bottle back. But only on his terms. His condition was that if we ordered another bottle – another Dom Perignon or any other wine – he would not accept any complaints and would not replace it under any circumstances. TCA can spread from one cork to another so I was not going to risk another DP from the same case. We ordered a different sparkling wine and it was fine. I didn't leave a tip and never went back there again.

A few months later and a rather different corked wine experience in a Leeds restaurant, this one specialising in modern British food.

I had arranged to have dinner with an eminent and outspoken wine journalist. We went to Heathcotes, a restaurant in a converted grain warehouse sitting astride the Leeds-Liverpool canal south of the city centre.

I asked my guest to pick whatever he fancied from the wine list. He grinned when he spotted Château d'Yquem, a legendary sweet white wine from the Sauternes region in south west France. This is arguably the best sweet wine in the world, certainly one of the best and one of the priciest. I was surprised when he told me that he had never tasted it, and I ordered a half bottle to go with dessert.

Château d'Yquem (pronounced dee-kem) has a lovely flavour like rich orange marmalade. But we didn't get that. We got the horrible dank, mouldy aroma and flavour instead. I looked with apprehension at the waiter and prepared myself for another war of the corked super wines.

I shouldn't have worried. The waiter didn't even ask to taste the wine. He smelt it and immediately agreed with us, apologised profusely for the problem, and hurried of to get a replacement bottle. Unbelievably, it too was corked. The waiter smelt it, agreed again, apologised some more, and brought us a third bottle. Yet another dud. The TCA had infected a whole batch of corks. Clearly this was not going to be the evening my guest would experience the delights of Château d'Yquem. We applied the 'three strikes and you're out' rule and ordered coffee. The restaurant had dealt with the problem beautifully and I tipped handsomely.

Unless you know what to look for, spotting a corked wine is not always easy. The mouldy flavour varies in intensity from full power to barely registering, like the energy test for a battery. When the mouldy flavour is very strong, the wine tastes quite disgusting. When it is mild, you may not realise it's there. It's not dangerous, so you might think it doesn't matter. You would be wrong. Even when mild, the mouldy character smothers the true flavour of the wine, subduing the taste. It's like listening to music with the volume turned down too low. You don't get the full impact.

I experienced this one evening in a Loch Fyne fish restaurant in London with a group of friends. Considering me the 'wine expert' they automatically chucked the wine list my way. I chose a Muscadet produced near Nantes in the Loire valley in north-west France, a region close to the fishing industry whose wines go well with the catch. After ordering it I went outside to make a call.

When I got back, our glasses had been filled. I asked the others what they thought of the wine. "Alright," was the general comment. I had been expecting a more enthusiastic response. Sure enough, when I took a sip the wine was corked. Not screamingly corked like the Château d'Yquem in Leeds, but enough to turn down the volume and hide the fruit flavours of the grapes. I asked for a replacement which was brought without question and it was fine. "Wow," was the reaction from my friends. "That's so much nicer," said one. "So much more flavour," said another. "I would never have realised," said a third.

And there lies the problem. Taste is personal and we don't all experience it in the same way. Some of us are very sensitive to the mouldy, wet cardboard flavours created by a bad cork, others not. My friends didn't realise the first bottle of Muscadet was corked. They just thought it was a style of wine they didn't like too much. They were bowled over by the difference when they tasted the second.

There is no magic way round this problem. Being aware of it is a great start. Stick your nose in the glass and have a good sniff. Take a swig, keep it in your mouth and think about the taste. Fruity and alive? Pass. Flat, cardboard, dank? Fail.

If mouldy smells and wet cardboard flavours sound familiar to you, become a leader and speak up every time you taste a corked wine. It isn't in anyone's interest for faulty wines to go unnoticed or unchallenged.

Above all, don't be shy. A wine that is corked is a faulty product. Return it to the shop or the waiter and INSIST on a replacement. Good places want happy customers and will take it back. Bad places which refuse to take it back don't deserve any customers. Put them on Facebook and Tripadvisor.

IN ONE GULP

When a cork is infected by the chemical TCA it imparts mouldy, dank flavours to the wine, spoiling the flavour. A wine whose flavour has been spoilt in this way is said to be 'corked'. The degree of 'corkiness' varies from mild to very strong. A corked wine is a faulty product. Always return it and ask for a replacement.

Why do some wines have corks and others have screwcaps?

At the turn of the millennium only the cheapest plonk was sold in bottles with screwcaps. They were short, ugly, mean little devices, notoriously difficult to open and good at scratching fingers.

Today the frog has turned into a prince. Everything in the screwcap universe has changed. 95% of wines from New Zealand and 75% from Australia are sealed in bottles with screw-caps. Every wine-producing country has caught on, and the shelves of UK supermarkets are filled with them.

Why did wine producers turn away from corks? 'Corked' wine was the reason. The chemical TCA that can infect one in 15 bottles and give the wine an off flavour is bad for business. Retailers, wholesalers and producers lost money refunding bottles because they were 'off'. Brands lost future sales to consumers who didn't like the wine and were not aware the bottle was faulty. Plastic corks were tried but the difficulty of getting them back into the bottle made them unpopular. Screwcaps seized the opportunity.

Today's screwcaps are a far cry from their cheap predecessors. New versions have been developed that protect the quality of the wine in the bottle very well. They have high-tech internal linings and long 'skirts' which have been tested over many years. The trials prove they work well for all types of wine – white, rosé and red. They keep the wine much as it tasted the day it was put in the bottle and have one huge advantage: the wine cannot be tainted by an infected cork.

Not for the first time in the modern winemaking era, the Australians led the way. Development of the modern screwcap started in the mid 1970s, but it was not until 2000 that producers in the Clare Valley used them on bottles of their famous Riesling wines and the momentum went up a gear. Their 'Riesling with a Twist' campaign was a clarion call for change. In 2002 it was taken up in the UK by Tesco who saw – or more accurately made – the future by launching a range of 26 wines in screwcap. Today they are used on wines from all over the world.

But it's not game over for corks, not by a long way. Acceptance of screwcaps is culturally sensitive. Producers in the traditional wine countries of Europe are less open to change than those in the southern hemisphere. Most consumers in the UK now accept screwcaps, but in many other countries they do not; the power of tradition means cork rules. The biggest obstacle to screwcaps gaining further ground is psychological – a bottle with a cork just feels nicer. Many people think expensive wines should have a cork because it gives a more prestigious image.

The debate between cork and screwcap boils down to four main issues: quality, convenience, romance and the environment.

QUALITY

The cork industry won't agree that the war has been lost, but most of the battles over quality have been won by the modern 'Stelvin' screwcaps.

There was a belief that screwcaps were not good for red wines, or for any wines that needed to be stored for 10 years or more. Studies and trials increasingly disprove these doubts. If anything, they show that the seal of high-quality screwcaps keeps wines better for longer. For long term storage bottles with corks should be kept lying down to prevent the cork from drying out, whereas those with screwcaps can be stored any way.

For 99% of wines - the majority that are drunk within a few weeks of purchase and anyway within a year or two – screwcaps provide constant, reliable quality.

Spurred on by this commercial threat, the cork industry undertook extensive research and development aimed at eradicating TCA from their product. The largest producer of cork products in the world claims to have done just that. The website of Portuguese company Amorim declares that "the company can safely say that it has beaten TCA – today, releasable TCA levels in Amorim cork stoppers are undetectable".

This is great news for Amorim's products. However corked wines still appear with alarming frequency. There is a wide range of corks in use – from low to high grade, cheap to expensive, short to long – with considerable quality variation between them. For the time being at least, the risk of the flavour being ruined by a bad cork remains.

CONVENIENCE

Screwcap wins hands down. No need for a corkscrew; no more struggling to get an impossibly tight cork out; no more chopping slivers off the end to make the cork fit back into an unfinished bottle. Just twist off and on. Waiters in busy restaurants love them for their ease and time-saving.

ROMANCE

Cork wins every time. The tradition of pulling a cork adds a touch of class and romance. The pop sends a message of anticipation to our brain. Get ready, enjoyment is coming. By contrast screwcaps are dull and functional. Efforts were made to develop a popping sound as the cap comes off. To date we are still waiting.

ENVIRONMENT

The cork industry argues that cork is better for the environment. They have backing from the World Wildlife Fund and the Forest Stewardship Council.

The largest areas of cork oak forest are in Western Mediterranean countries: Portugal, Spain, Italy, France, Morocco, Tunisia and Algeria. The world produces 340,000 tonnes of cork a year, 55% of which is from Portugal. The production of cork products does not involve cutting down the trees. The bark is removed every 9 to 12 years, leading to a process of self-regeneration, and some trees live for up to 300 years.

Cork trees capture carbon dioxide (CO_2), provide jobs, and are beneficial to wildlife. Species include the Iberian lynx, the Barbary deer and the Egyptian mongoose, as well as rare birds such as the Iberian imperial eagle and the black stork.

Amorim says that, even without taking into account the CO_2 captured by cork oak forests, greenhouse gas emissions associated with cork stoppers are 24 times lower than those recorded for aluminium closures, and 10 times lower than those made of plastic.

On the other hand, supporters of screwcaps point out that many cork forests are not ethically managed, that the energy used in making a recyclable aluminium screwcap is significantly less than is used in making a cork, and that although corks can in theory be recycled there is no system to do so in the UK so most end up in landfill, while metal screwcaps are processed by normal recycling systems.

TECHNOLOGICAL PROGRESS

Someone whose livelihood depended on driving a coach and horses was never going to welcome Henry Ford's new motor vehicle. There is a similar feeling about the cork industry's response to screwcaps. To keep their business sustainable cork producers need to match the benefits of screwcaps, or develop alternative products and markets.

The screwcap versus cork debate is at root one of technology. So it's pertinent to ask this question: If wine had only just been discovered as a drink, would the packaging designers use a piece of tree to seal the container it comes in? It's unlikely.

Until the 17th century wine was kept in containers sealed by cloth soaked in olive oil, or pieces of wood or glass. Then cork was discovered to be a superior method. It was the new technology of the time. Four centuries later the new has become old, and the cycle is being repeated.

IN ONE GULP

Corks were first used to seal wine bottles centuries ago when they were the best technology available. They have become part of the tradition and ritual of wine. But the problem of 'corked' wines ruins many bottles. For wine quality and convenience, screwcaps are a better modern solution.

How long will wine Keep in an open bottle?

The usual answer to this question is "Not more than half an hour round at our house!" Finishing the bottle certainly ensures you drink the wine while it's fresh. But for those rare occasions when a night with friends leaves a bottle unfinished, or you've had a glass or two on your own, there are alternatives.

Oxygen changes wine. For a few hours after the wine has been opened and poured, the oxygen gets in and 'releases' the flavour. This is a good thing. But the oxygen keeps working away and after about 24 hours the taste begins to lose freshness, until weeks later it tastes vinegary.

A normal half-full bottle of wine with a cork or screwcap which is kept in the fridge (reds too) will taste OK for up to three days. 'OK' doesn't mean identical to when it was opened, but nice enough to drink. Wine quality does not turn on and off like a light switch, but changes gradually like the tide. As oxygen gets a grip, the flavours begin to fade and dull, until eventually they die.

The secret to preserving good flavours in an opened bottle is to keep the oxygen out and the temperature down. The more you follow this rule the longer it will last.

WHAT NOT TO DO

- Don't leave the top off the bottle at the end of the evening

- Don't leave the bottle out in the kitchen, living room or any warm place. Heat hastens the chemical process that changes the taste

- Don't keep the bottle on its side. This exposes more surface of the wine to air

- Don't expect as good results from a bottle that is almost empty as one that is almost full. Wine and air are in a zero sum game. Less wine means more air, making it harder to stay fresh

FOR BEST RESULTS

Keep the wine in a sealed bottle standing up in the fridge. If your fridge is big enough, keep it on a shelf. If it's in the door, the wine and air slosh around a bit every time it is opened.

For better results, separate the wine from the air altogether. A great method is to pour it into a small empty mineral water bottle. Keep 25cl, 33cl and 50cl rinsed plastic bottles ready and fill them as close to the top as possible, screw the cap on, and put them in the fridge. If the bottles are full the wine will keep for many weeks – as long as it hasn't already been sitting around open by the cooker for ages.

If the wine you have stored in the fridge is red take the chill off it before drinking by standing the bottle in warm water. For quicker results take the top off the bottle, stand it in a bowl, and give it a short spin in the micro-wave. Short spin means a few seconds not minutes.

If the DIY option doesn't appeal to you, there are several commercial devices that aim to separate wine from oxygen. Vacu Vin pumps the air out and has been around for many years. It works but only for two or three days, much the same as resealing with screwcap or cork, except that the wine quality and fresh flavours should be better preserved.

Private Preserve works by injecting a layer of harmless gas (a mixture of carbon dioxide, nitrogen and argon) that creates a protective layer over the wine. It keeps the wine good for much longer and works on any quantity left in the bottle, even a glassful. One user on the company's website reports a half bottle of Cabernet Sauvignon tasting as good as new after six months. With consistently excellent reviews this seems to be the choice of the moment.

Coravin is a device targeting expensive bottles of wine. It allows you to drink a glass at a time over many months. A medical grade needle pierces the cork and inserts Argon gas into the bottle when wine is poured out. It's far from cheap but apparently works well.

For longer-term storage use the freezer. Put the wine in a plastic mineral water bottle with enough space for it to expand a little. It will keep for many months. Once defrosted the wine should be nice and fresh. If you need to defrost in a hurry carefully use the microwave. Don't be alarmed if you find crystals or a powdery like residue at the bottom of your glass. They are usually removed by the chilling or storage process when wine is made, but may otherwise 'fall out' when the wine is frozen. They are natural and harmless.

If there is only a little wine left in the bottle, fill some ice cube shapes and freeze them. These are good to suck as refreshing wine cubes or to use in sauces.

BAG-IN-BOX

In Sweden 55% of all wine is sold in Bag-in-Box. In the UK we associate them with the cheapest wines, but the quality has been rising in recent years. A friend of mine has a supermarket Chilean Sauvignon Blanc bag-in-box on tap in her fridge at all times. This is unremarkable until you know that she is a Master of Wine, the top nerd qualification there is in the wine trade. If bag-in-box is good enough for Fiona, it's good enough for me.

A box may not look as attractive as a bottle, but their system of keeping wine fresh is much better. Because the bag has no air in it, the wine lasts for six to eight weeks once opened. Apart from their higher cost and larger size – traditionally 3 litres, the equivalent of 4 bottles, but also 2.25 litres or 3 bottles – I wonder why we don't buy more of them. They have the advantage of being much lighter than glass, and are responsible for fewer carbon dioxide emissions per litre when transported commercially.

I once suggested to our New Product Development team that we design a bag-in-box with a see-through column, making it easy to know how much wine was left inside. The whole group looked at me as though I was from another planet. Then one of them explained that this would reduce rather than increase sales, because many people buy a bag-in-box so their partner doesn't know how much they are drinking.

CHAMPAGNE AND SPARKLING WINE

Keeping bubbly alive is different. The only proven method to preserve bubbles and freshness is to use one of the special pressure resisting clip-on Champagne corks. As always, keep the wine in the fridge. In my experience, the next day is good; the one after that is very much touch and go.

The old wives' tales don't work. The idea that an upside-down spoon in the bottle neck will preserve the fizz is a dud. Some people get excited by the restorative powers of raisins. They believe dropping two or three into a bottle that has lost its fizz will get the bubbles bouncing again. Others think putting a raisin in a glass before filling it with wine from an overnight bottle works even better.

Alas the joy, if any, is short-lived. The raisin can't create additional bubbles – it's just a raisin – but it can attract the remaining carbon dioxide and then release it. Once the bubbles have been released, the wine is even flatter than before. What does create a show is doing the same when the bubbly is fresh and fizzy. The raisin bobs up and down in the glass as it attracts and then releases the carbon dioxide.

IN ONE GULP

A partially-empty bottle left open overnight will be losing its freshness by the next morning. Kept in the fridge with the cork or screwcap on it will last for up to 3 days. Transferred to completely fill a small plastic bottle it can last for several weeks.

Is it true that wines improve with age?

You can waste a lot of money with wine if you don't know what you are doing. Unhappily I am speaking from experience.

My first wine business dealt mostly in organic wines. One of my favourites was a red Côtes du Rhône called Vignoble de la Jasse made by Daniel Combe. The second time we shipped his wine over from France I bought two cases for myself and stored them in the basement of my house. I assumed the wine could only improve. When I opened the bottles five years later they weren't better; they were undrinkable. I poured all 24 down the sink.

Virtually all wines on sale in supermarkets and shops today are ready to drink immediately. Most have been made in the last two years and the producers know the wines will be drunk within a few weeks, days, or even hours of being purchased. Older wines like Rioja Reserva are kept by the producer until they are ready to drink before being released for sale. Either way, once the bottles are in the shops, they are meant to be drunk.

None of these wines will improve with age. They may hold their quality for a while before they get worse – how long varies from wine to wine as I found out to my cost with the Côtes du Rhône – but the best advice is to drink up and buy afresh when you need.

In the past, winemaking was not as sophisticated or as commercially focused as it is today. Red wines often tasted tough and tannic, and leaving them to change chemically in the bottle for several years made them softer and easier to drink. This led to the idea that older was better. Specialist wine merchants still sell some red wines, notably from France and Italy, that need to age for a few more years to be at their best for drinking, as well as some white wines that are several years old and still tasting as their maker intended. Such wines are almost always expensive.

But generally, these days, we want our wines tasting of ripe, juicy flavours. And we want them now. Grape-growing and winemaking have evolved to give us this.

Everyday white and rosé wines are at their most delicious when they have lots of lively fresh fruit, so younger is better. Avoid those that are more than a couple of years old like the plague. Red wines keep their quality better for longer, with full-bodied, heavier wines tending to last better than light ones, but there is nothing to be gained in hanging on to either.

Here is how to avoid the worst pitfalls and drink your wine at its best:

Read what is written on the back label about how long the wine will last.

Don't panic if there is sediment in the wine. It probably means the wine has been made without too much filtration, which is usually a good thing for retaining the flavour. However, if the wine is more than five years old sediment can be a sign of age. A lot of solid matter in an old wine may be a sign that the colour and flavour are going too.

Stay on your guard. Bottle size affects how quickly a wine ages. Half bottles age faster than normal 75cl bottles, and 150cl magnums age more slowly. Never, ever do what I did and buy a half bottle of Spanish rosé in a restaurant in Majorca. No-one else ever bought this size (they sensibly chose 75cl) and my bottle had been quietly dying during the years it lingered in the store room. It was an uninviting brown colour by the time it arrived at our table, and tasted as bad as it looked.

Stay constant. If you plan to keep wines for more than a few weeks, put them somewhere where the temperature doesn't go up and down like a yoyo. Dramatic temperature change kills flavour. Next to the oven, dishwasher or drier is not good. The airing cupboard is a disaster.

The 18-20°C of today's central heating is fine for wines that are drunk within a few weeks, but for long-term storage a constant 13-14°C is recommended. An Italian study compared bottles of red Sangiovese stored in a professional cellar at a constant 15-16°C with the same wine in typical home conditions with temperatures varying between 20-26°C. After 6 months the home bottles were found to have an inferior taste and to have 'aged' four times faster than those in the professional cellar.

When you drink red wine remember that the idea of serving it at 'room temperature' dates back centuries, long before central heating existed. In those days the temperature in people's houses was much lower than today.

Stay dark. We like sunlight, but wine doesn't. The coloured glass of a wine bottle acts like its sunglasses, protecting it from the rays. It's best to store bottles – especially clear glass – away from direct light of any kind, and ideally in the dark. Putting them directly under a light bulb, which also gives off heat, is a red card offence.

Don't be colour blind. If you're unsure about how long a wine will keep, look at the colour. Unless it happens to be in a clear bottle this means pouring some into a glass, by which time it's too late to keep it, so this really only works if you have more than one bottle of the same wine. Wines get darker and duller as they get older. Whites become more yellow and ultimately brown. Reds start purple when they are young, move to brick-red in middle age, and turn brown when the end is nigh.

But watch out. Wines start with different hues of colour when they are first made. You only need to look at the light green, almost watery colour of an Italian Pinot Grigio against the deep yellow of an oak-aged Australian Chardonnay to see the contrast. In this case the Chardonnay is not darker because it is older; it's just its character. A darker colour in a young white wine usually signifies a stronger flavour and vice versa.

If you buy wines from a shop with a regular sales turnover, there should not be a problem with them being too old. But if you have several bottles of a brick-red wine at home, get the corkscrew out fast.

IN ONE GULP

The vast majority of the wines on sale are ready for immediate drinking. They will not improve with age. How quickly they will deteriorate depends on the wine. White and rosé generally lose freshness and quality faster than red.

Why does wine cost so much?

What do you think is the average price paid for a bottle of wine in a shop? £7? £8? £9? My guess is that the number you have in mind is too high. In 2016 it was around £5.40. The higher prices seen on the shelves are brought tumbling down by the large quantity sold at a promotional discount. So what are you getting for your money?

Here's a breakdown of costs in a £5 bottle (2017 figures):

- **Tax:** Alcohol tax and VAT account for £2.99 of the £5. That's almost 60%.

- **Retailer:** Assuming a profit margin of 30% of the sale price (after deducting VAT) the retailer gets £1.25.

- **Everything else:** That leaves 76p to cover the wine in the bottle, the bottle itself, the cork or screwcap, labels, carton, and transporting it from where it is made to your local store. And if the retailer buys the wine from a distributor, rather than direct from the winery, it includes the distributor's margin too.

It is astonishing how little of the £5 goes on the liquid itself. The six glasses of wine in a bottle could cost as little as 40p – that's just 7p a glass for the producer in France, Chile or wherever. And it's drinkable stuff. So let's delve deeper into why there is such an enormous gulf between the price on the shelf and the cost at the winery door.

TAX
UK alcohol duty (tax) on a bottle of wine is fixed. At £2.16 a bottle it is a juicy 43% of a £5 bottle, 22% at £10 and only 7% at £30. The higher the price, the lower the proportion that goes to the Government. This makes more expensive wines seem relatively better value, with more of what you spend going on the wine. They may be so, but not necessarily. It all depends on why the wine costs more.

RETAILER PROFIT MARGINS

Retailers have different profit margins. One may take 15% of the sale price and another 50%. Most are somewhere in the middle. Assume that two retailers with different profit margins buy a wine at the same cost from a supplier. If one has a 20% margin and the other 40%, the price on the shelf of the 40% retailer will be higher. In this case the higher cost means that more is going to the retailer, not to the wine producer.

The same is true the other way round. If both retailers sell wines at say £8, the retailer who takes 40% of the sale price as his margin must be paying less for their wine than the retailer who only takes 20%.

It's logical to think that the wine selling for £8 in the 20% retailer will be better value, simply because they paid more for it. But costing more does not necessarily mean the wine is better. The extra may be taken up by the producer having a less efficient business operation, or a bigger profit margin, or because they are in a high cost production area.

GETTING IT THERE

One of the most significant factors in the cost of any product is the 'supply chain'. This is the number of stages it has to go through between the place of production and the shelf in the store or the delivery to your home. Every time there is another stage in the supply chain, the cost goes up.

If a big retailer sends a truck to France to collect 16,000 bottles of wine from the producer, or contracts a shipping company to bring them in a container from Australia, it's an A to B operation between where the wine is made and where it is sold. The supply chain is said to be short and the extra costs per bottle are low. (It's a bizarre fact that, despite the enormous difference in distance, the costs of transport by road from France and by boat from Australia are much the same.)

But if a wholesaler brings wine to the UK from France or Australia, pays to store it in a warehouse, then pays for delivery of a few cases to a small shop, the supply chain is long and the additional costs are high. The wholesaler, warehouse and delivery company all need to add their margin. On top of which small shops usually need a higher margin than a supermarket.

The difference between these two 'routes to market' is crucial in determining the retail price. It's often more significant than the cost of the wine itself.

A wine that goes directly from winery to supermarket might sell for £6.99, while the same wine going through the long supply chain may be £9.99 in an independent shop. That's why most independent shops don't want to sell the same brands as the big retailers.

THE DIFFERENCE BETWEEN EVERYDAY AND EXPENSIVE WINES

The vast majority of wines sold are everyday wines. We buy them like other groceries and drink them as habitually as Coke or coffee. They sell for less than £10 and make up over 98% of wine sold in UK shops. It's hardly surprising that the market for these wines is fiercely competitive and that cost is king.

Wine geeks may not like to hear it, but from a commercial point of view one £7 Australian Shiraz, Chilean Chardonnay or French Côtes du Rhône is much the same as the next. Of course there are taste differences between different brands, but the general type is usually very similar. You only have to ask for a glass of white wine in a bar and be offered Pinot Grigio or Sauvignon Blanc without the bar person mentioning the brand, or even the country, to experience how generalised the market has become. If one particular Pinot Grigio or Sauvignon Blanc becomes unavailable, or too expensive, another will quickly take its place. In this market the wine producer has little choice but to sell their wine as cheaply as they can afford to do, and sometimes for less than that.

Expensive wines work in a different context and to different rules. The price of wines that sell for £15 or more, and especially those at much higher prices, is less to do with what they cost to produce and more with what the producer feels they can get. Rather than competing on price to sell huge volumes, expensive wines do the opposite. They are made in limited quantities and use their scarcity value and prestige to command a high price. Then the price becomes part of the image – it's expensive, so it must be good. The famous Châteaux of Bordeaux that sell for hundreds or thousands of pounds a bottle are at the top of this pile. As demand goes up, so does their price.

RESTAURANTS

Like independent shops, restaurants are at the end of a long supply chain. The bottle passes through a lot of hands between a small winery in New Zealand's South Island and an independent restaurant in Edinburgh. As restaurants don't want their cash tied up in mountains of stock, they usually buy from wholesalers who can deliver a few cases every day. It all costs money.

Most restaurants sell wine for between three and four times the price they pay for it. This is a much higher mark-up than in shops. Customers resent paying £25 in a restaurant if they can buy the same bottle for £7 in the local supermarket or shop. That's why it's rare to see the same labels in both. It's also why some wine producers have two different labels for the same wine.

THE COST OF MAKING WINE

Wine has a glamorous feel to it. But for most of the 50,000 wineries in the world, remaining economically viable is a daily battle. Though we might think of winemaking as a creative and artistic activity, like painting or music, it's essentially farming.

The process falls into two stages – growing the grapes, and turning them into wine. What comes next is the hard bit – selling the wine at a profit.

The cost of producing grapes depends on three main factors: the land the vineyard is planted on, the cost of labour, and the quantity of grapes produced. High-cost land and labour combined with low-quantity production leads to expensive grapes. Low-cost land and labour combined with high-quantity production leads to cheap grapes. The interplay of these factors explains why different countries, and different regions within the same country, produce wines with very different prices.

Once the grapes have been picked, the techniques used to process them into wine differ in cost. Apart from the equipment and materials used in the winery, whether or not expensive oak barrels are used to ferment or store the wine is a major factor.

How long the wines are kept before they are sold is crucial. Financing stock eats up cash. A fast turnaround white or rosé made from grapes picked in August might be bottled and sold in December. That's good for cash flow. Most everyday wine producers aim to have their stock of white and rosé sold before the following year's wine is ready. This has two advantages – they get their cash back relatively quickly, and the wines are drunk while still fresh and at their best.

On the other hand, a red wine that is left to age in oak barrels for months – or years – in order to let the flavours evolve has far greater costs. A friend in the Lirac region of the southern Rhône valley in France makes red wines that are not noticeably oaky in taste, but she would not dream of selling a bottle until at least 18 months after the harvest. She wants the wines to develop certain flavours before her customers drink them.

Some regions are obliged by their local rules to keep the wine for a specified amount of time before they can sell it. In Rioja, the use of the word Reserva on red wines is only allowed if it has been kept for three years, and in oak barrels for at least one of those years. Time and barrels cost money, so the wines sell at a higher price. (Ridiculously, in many other countries the word Reserva has no specific meaning and is used purely as a marketing tool.)

You might expect the poorest countries to produce the cheapest wines. But this is not always true. Land and labour are cheaper in areas like Eastern Europe and North Africa than in France or America, but they often lack the wine industry infrastructure and support services that create efficiency and bring down prices.

Finally, there is size. Small-scale craftsman-style wines cost more to produce than those from factories that churn out millions of bottles, just as artisan handmade shoes cost more than Clarks, and farm shop jams cost more than Robertson's.

WHERE YOUR MONEY GOES

The illustration below shows where your money goes at different retail prices. It is based on wine sold in a supermarket or other major retailer. Retailer and distributor margins vary from company to company, and delivery costs depend on the type of supply chain used, so the numbers are indicative rather than precise. The category of 'everything else' includes the price paid to the winery for the bottle of wine as well as transport costs, distributor margin and, where applicable, UK storage.

	£4.99	£6.99	£8.99	£11.99
Retailer Margin	25%	30%	30%	30%
Government Taxes	60%	48%	41%	35%
Everything Else	15%	22%	29%	35%

IN ONE GULP

Under £10 the wine itself is a relatively small part of the price you pay for a bottle. Alcohol tax and VAT take a big portion. Retailer and distributor margins account for most of the rest.

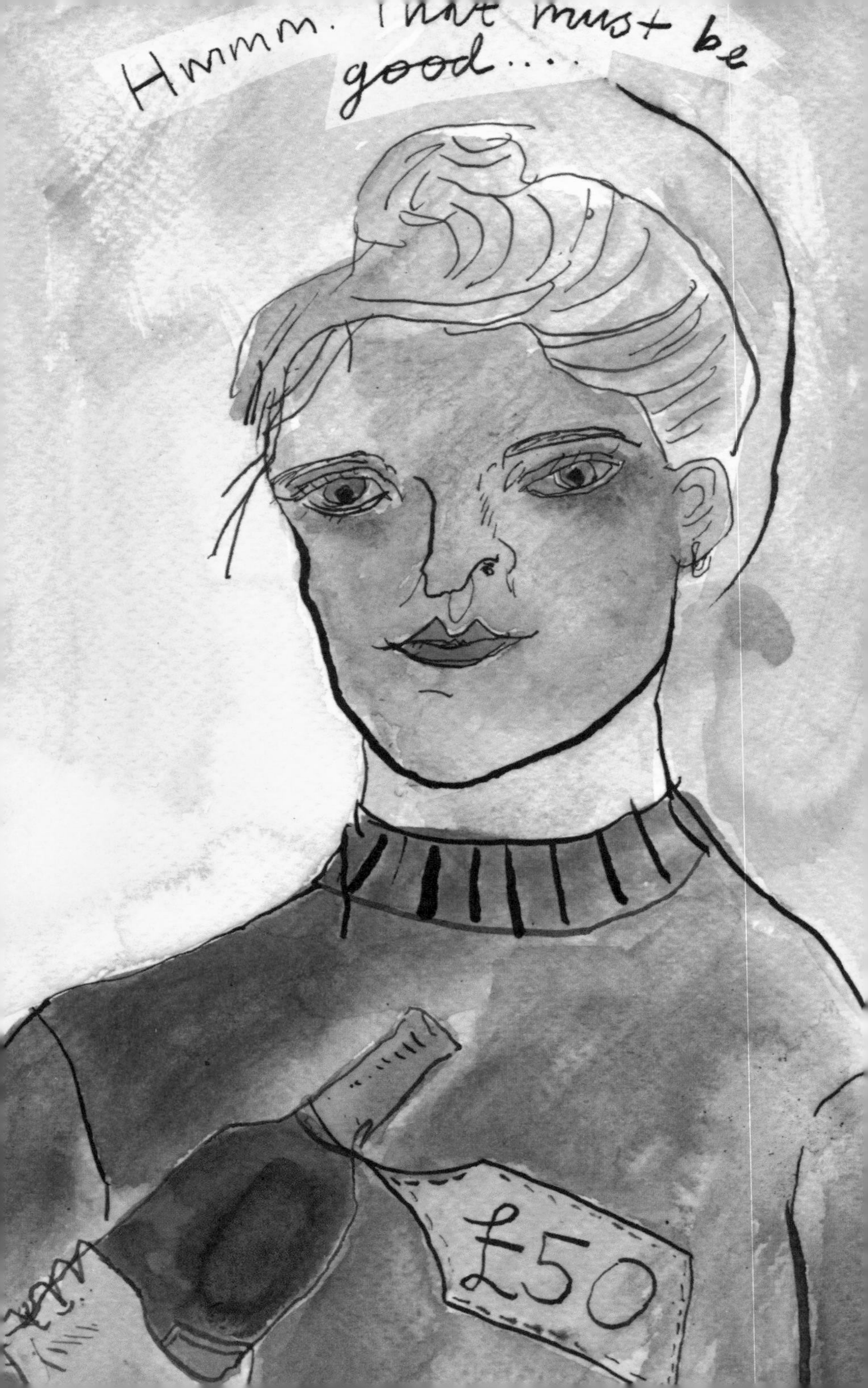
Hmmm. That must be good....
£50

Do more expensive wines always taste better?

This is a great question. The answer reveals as much about us as it does about wine.

In 2001 French researcher Frédéric Brochet conducted an experiment with 54 winemaking students to test their perceptions of differently priced wines. He gave the students two red wines to taste, with an interval of a week between them. One was an expensive Bordeaux in a fancy bottle, the other a cheap table wine in a plain bottle. Unsurprisingly, the majority of the students much preferred the more expensive wine.

But it was a trick. The wine in the bottles was the same – a middle-priced Bordeaux. The students' interpretation of the taste was fashioned by their preconceptions based on the look of the bottle and assumptions about the price. They tasted what they were expecting to taste.

Brochet's experiment is one of several to show that we taste with our eyes and our minds before our taste buds. Our opinions are influenced by all sorts of things that are nothing to do with the liquid itself. One of the most powerful is price. If you know a wine is expensive you are predisposed to think it must be good. But when all the influences are removed, most people cannot tell an expensive wine from a cheap one.

During a 'blind tasting' – when the drinkers have no idea what the wine is – at the Edinburgh Science Festival 578 people tasted wines ranging from cheap (£5 or less) to expensive (£10-30). When asked to say whether they thought the wine they were drinking was cheap or expensive, on average their ability to tell was no better than flipping a coin.

Similarly a study of 6,000 blind tastings in the USA found there was no correlation between what people liked and high price. If anything, it showed that people enjoyed the more expensive wines slightly less. The authors concluded :

"Our results indicate that both the prices of wines and wine recommendations by experts may be poor guides for non-expert wine consumers."

This was borne out in a report from the London Wine Academy, where 80% of drinkers preferred a £4.99 Australian Chardonnay to a £19.99 French Burgundy (also made with Chardonnay grapes), and 60% thought the cheaper of the two was the more expensive.

Even wine experts struggle to match taste and price. A tasting in the USA between some of the most expensive Châteaux in France and wines from New Jersey – not a historically renowned American wine region – was won by the French, but only by the smallest of margins. The American wines were judged to be virtually on a par with the French for quality but were a lot cheaper – sometimes as little as 10% of the price.

The results are clear. When they do not know what the wine is, most people cannot tell which is cheap and which is expensive. They are at least as likely to prefer cheaper wine. However, when they do know what it is, they prefer the more expensive wine – or what they believe to be expensive.

There are two things going on here: the wine in the bottle and our perception about what we are drinking. The wine is what it is. But how we interpret the taste is affected by a wide array of influences including what other people say, the price, what the bottle looks like, the environment, and our mood.

The previous chapter showed that paying a few pounds more is no guarantee of getting a 'better' wine. One wine costs more than another for a host of reasons, many unrelated to quality. Most significantly, quality and 'better' are questions of personal taste.

Nor is it surprising that people prefer the easy-drinking taste of cheaper wines. Expensive wines tend to be more difficult to drink, especially the reds. Getting to like them takes effort. If you attend a wine course that explains what to look for in the taste, practise a lot and think about it you may – perhaps – come to prefer them. But without such training it is normal that everyday wines get most people's vote.

American Tim Hanni suggests people can be divided into four wine types. Once we know our "Vinotype" we can choose wines that will correspond to our preferences. Hanni says our individual taste is determined by a combination of the genetics we were born with and what we absorb through culture, learning and environment. Our likes and dislikes in wine reflect our personality and preferences in other areas of life too. So by knowing the answer to questions such as whether we like bitter black coffee or really hate noisy restaurants he can build up a picture of our "sensitivities and values", including the type and range of wine we will like. It makes a lot of sense. Try his short questionnaire on myvinotype.com – it's pretty revealing.

So, is there ever a reason to splash out on a more expensive wine? I think there is.

First, while on average people can't tell the difference between cheap and expensive wines, averages are made up of many different opinions and you may be someone who just prefers the taste of more expensive styles – even when you taste them blind. The only way to find out is to try.

Second, we do not drink wine in a vacuum. We drink it in real-life situations. If you were drinking an expensive wine on a special occasion – for example, when you proposed to your partner, or when your sports team became champion – that wine may taste fantastic to you forever. Wine is at its very best when it stirs good emotions and memories.

Third, the very fact that it costs more can be positive. If I am going round to a friend's for dinner, I don't want to take a £5 bottle even if it tastes good to me. I want to feel I have bought something a bit special so I want to spend more. It makes me feel right. I will feel even better if my friend realises I have brought along a more expensive wine. There is a good chance it will then taste better to both of us.

This is not as nuts as it sounds. The context and message affect our appreciation of the liquid.

Fourth, expensive wines often come from smaller, less commercial producers with great stories to tell. Maybe they gave up a good salary as a dentist to live the dream, sinking their life savings into a rundown winery with a wrecked vineyard in the back of beyond. Or maybe you stopped at the winery gate as you drove past on holiday and now, every time you sip a glass of their wine, you think of them ploughing the fields by horse. Connecting with people and their stories makes the wine taste much more interesting.

Of course, whether a wine is expensive or not is a relative thing. £25 is nothing to a multi-millionaire, but it's a fortune to someone living on the state pension. With the average price between £5 and £6, and 98% of all bottles sold costing under £10, the market is saying that anything north of £10 is expensive. This is confirmed in specialist wine merchants where only a handful of wines are under £10 and their clients rarely spend less than £15, and usually a lot more.

The reason wines in this price bracket cost so much boils down to three things: production cost, scarcity and prestige.

Expensive wines are usually made from vines that produce fewer grapes which, because there are less of them, have a greater intensity of flavour. As discussed in the last chapter, fewer grapes, using oak barrels and keeping the wine for a long time before selling it lead to higher cost.

But the higher cost of producing premium wines does not fully explain the high price on the shelf. Most are made in limited quantities and this scarcity allows them to develop an exclusive image. When a winery develops a prestigious reputation for its top-of-the-range products and combines it with scarcity, silly prices can result.

These three things – production cost, scarcity and prestige – drive up price, and can also make a wine taste better, more interesting and more memorable.

I was lucky enough to be invited to a 50th birthday lunch where the host spotted a bottle of Château d'Yquem 1963 on the wine list. He was born in

1963 and knew a lot about wine. When he saw it cost 'only' £600 a bottle there was never any doubt about the outcome. Château d'Yquem is probably the greatest dessert wine in the world and £600 was cheap for a 50 year old bottle in a restaurant. The wine was dark brown, tasted of mince pies and was as fresh as a daisy. I shall remember the experience for the rest of my life.

Do more expensive wines always taste better? Absolutely not. But sometimes they do, especially when there is a story to 'taste' as well.

IN ONE GULP

More expensive wines do not always taste better. Taste is personal. There is no simple correlation between the cost of a wine and how much someone will enjoy it. In blind taste tests people often prefer cheaper wines.

Are heavily discounted wines worth the full price?

Most wine is bought in supermarkets, and most of that is bought at a discounted price. The promotions range from save £2, through 25% off, to half price. And we do love a bargain. Sales of a wine on half-price offer can increase by 100 times or more.

Price promotions attract customers and sell large volumes. The bigger the price reduction, the more is sold. Suppliers wanting to sell big volumes cut their cost price to the retailer for the promotional period. Retailers often also reduce their margins.

This works fine for the smaller discounts, such as £2 or 25% off. The supplier settles for selling at a lower price once or twice a year so that people notice their wine and give it a try. They may only break even on these sales, but they hope that someone who likes the wine will buy it again at the full price.

However for the really big promotional discounts, such as half price, the numbers don't seem to add up. A wine selling for £5 typically costs the supermarket around £1 to buy, the exact price depending on the foreign exchange rate and their profit margin. Transport from the winery, alcohol duty and VAT take the rest. Under the same conditions, a £10 wine costs around £3.40.

For a £10 wine to be promoted at £5 it looks as though the supplier needs to drop their cost from £3.40 to as little as £1, depending on how much the retailer's margin is reduced. Such a big drop is impossible for most suppliers without selling at a huge loss. So there has to be another way of achieving these half-price reductions.

The answer is for the retailer to buy low and sell high. A wine costing £1 can be sold at £10 and then reduced to £5 on promotion.

Critics cry foul. They accuse the supermarkets of selling mutton dressed as lamb, while also taking an abnormally large profit margin at the £10 price. They say that if a wine costs £1 it could, and should, be sold much cheaper.

They argue that when a wine is heavily discounted for large parts of the year, the discounted price is actually the 'real' price. They also say it makes no sense for wines costing £1 and others costing £3.40 to both be sold at £10.

In reply, retailers say that the wine has been carefully selected for quality and value. Good buying and modern winemaking skills mean a wine with a taste worth £10 can be made at a low cost. They also point to customer satisfaction with their range and promotional activity.

The question is how to measure a wine's worth. Is it about the price on the shelf, how much the retailer paid for it, and how much money they are making? Or is it nothing to do with that, but about how much we like the taste? As we all taste differently, how is that to be assessed?

These 3 responses to the same wine show it is not a simple issue:

Someone who buys a wine at £10 and enjoys it a lot is happy. Someone else who buys the same wine for £5 on half price promotion and doesn't like it is unhappy. A third person, also buying the wine at half price but liking it, enjoys the taste more because they got a bargain. In all three cases the price the retailer paid for the wine is irrelevant to the drinker's level of satisfaction.

The same applies to other big discounts, not just half price. A good test is to compare different wines of a similar type at a certain price – say £10 – some of which are frequently promoted at a heavy discount and others which are not. Drink them blind without knowing which is which. If the heavily promoted wines taste inferior to those that are not promoted in the same way, you will be in agreement with the critics. But if you like them as much – or more – not only are they worth £10, they're a steal on promotion.

Of course many wines are never discounted, especially those at lower prices. The £10/£5 wine could be sold at a constant price all year round instead. Taking into account the proportion sold and the profit margins at £10 and £5, the constant price would probably be around £5.99. The reason it isn't sold at this price all the time is because we would buy less of it. The 'theatre' of all those price discounts opens our wallets like nothing else.

Over 100 years ago, in 1892, one of Oscar Wilde's characters said "Nowadays people know the price of everything and the value of nothing." It seems that we are slow learners. If we stopped buying wines when the price was heavily discounted retailers would quickly stop offering them. In a world without price discounts we might focus more on the wine itself, which would be a good thing.

By and large we do not investigate the choice of wines available, try to understand the tastes and stories, decide what sounds appealing, and then look to see if any of those are on offer, buying one of our preferred styles anyway if they are not. Rather, we choose between red, white or rosé and let the promotional deal guide us.

Getting real value from wine requires a detox. It means breaking the addiction to the deal.

Decide how much you are prepared to spend and then look for wines you like within your price range, regardless of whether they are on offer or not. Consider the wine that is always sold at £5.99 in exactly the same way as one that is on promotion at £5.99. The price is the same. No matter which you buy, you will only get a penny change from £6. Judge the value of the wine on what you did pay rather than what you didn't, and above all on how much you enjoyed the taste.

IN ONE GULP

Interpretation of worth is personal. A wine is worth a particular price if you like it enough, it isn't if you don't. The answer is complicated for heavily discounted wines because we 'taste' the deal as well as the wine. Many could be sold at an intermediary constant price all year round. When they are we buy less.

Are supermarket own label wines any good?

Imagine that someone gives you three different glasses of Champagne to drink. One is a cheap supermarket own-label. Another is a well-known brand costing almost three times as much. The third is a special blend from a top producer costing ten times more.

You would expect the taste of the three times more expensive to be a lot better than the supermarket label, and for the ten times more to leave the others for dust. Otherwise why pay so much more? But when the three were compared in a competition this was not how it turned out. To make matters worse, it wasn't ordinary consumers who rocked the boat but wine tasting professionals.

Aldi's own-label Veuve Monsigny Champagne Brut by Philizot sells for £12.99. It won a Silver medal at the International Wine Challenge (IWC), putting it ahead of the £32.99 Moet & Chandon Imperial non-vintage and the £130 Veuve Clicquot La Grande Dame 2004.

Aldi are not the only supermarket whose buyers know how to ferret out a delicious drink and sell it under their own-label at a brand busting price. Tesco's Premier Cru Champagne sells for under £20 and has won a host of awards over the years including best Champagne at the IWC in 2005. Marks and Spencer's £10 Macon-Villages 2014 from Burgundy in France was chosen as the best Chardonnay in the world under £15 in the 2015 Decanter World Wine Awards.

Supermarket own-label wines won 498 medals at the IWC in 2015. Marks and Spencer, who sell virtually all their wines under the M&S label, grabbed the biggest haul. Charles Metcalfe, IWC co-chairman summed up the progress when he said:

"Supermarket buyers have demonstrated their talent for sourcing fantastic wines from all around the world, usually at pretty keen prices".

Of course the fact that a wine has won a medal doesn't mean that you or I will like it. Taste is personal. But the growing number of awards won by supermarket own-labels shows that they are doing increasingly well as a group against other wines presented.

It's really no surprise. Wickes' TV advertisement for their home improvement products has the voice of actor Timothy Spall reassuring us that we can trust them because "It's got our name on it. Wickes." He could just as well be talking about a supermarket and their own-label Cotes du Rhone, Australian Chardonnay or Chilean Merlot.

Supermarkets pay particular attention to the quality and style of products carrying their name because consumers' positive or negative responses are amplified. When we like one of their own-label wines it engenders a good feeling about them and their products in general. And we can only get more of it by shopping with them.

Equally, when we don't like one of their own-label wines the opposite happens, potentially damaging the whole relationship. Their nightmare is that we do our shopping somewhere else.

So it makes complete sense for supermarkets to put considerable effort into making sure their own-label wines are what they want them to be, and that consumers both like them and think they are good value. In most big retailers own-label is a minority of the wine range but it is strategically important.

Supermarkets began selling own label wines in 1973 with Marks and Spencer and Sainsbury's first away. Gradually every-one joined in. For many years they focused on lower priced better known wines such as Sainsbury's Cotes du Rhone, Asda Soave, Tesco Chilean Cabernet Sauvignon, or Waitrose Good Ordinary Claret. These were good value, reliable products, but largely unexciting.

Then came the idea of creating a 'ladder' or hierarchy within the own label wines, adding middle priced and higher priced levels. Tesco have the Simply range followed by Tesco and then Finest*; Sainsbury's have House, Taste the Difference and Winemakers Selection; Asda have Asda, Wine Selection and Extra Special; Morrison's have Morrison's and Signature. The names and hierarchy change over time but the principles of catering for all pockets and increasing consumer loyalty remain.

We are generally a pretty conservative bunch when it comes to choosing wine. Most of us don't risk buying something unfamiliar unless it is cheap or on offer or both. Efforts by independent brands to sell lesser known grape varieties such as Fiano or Touriga Nacional, regions such as Duoro or Toro, or countries such as Slovenia usually fail. The bottles gather dust on the shelves.

The success of the higher priced own label ranges offered a solution. The trust built up in Finest, Taste the Difference and others could be used to sell the lesser known grapes, regions and countries. The hope was that our confidence in the brand would overcome our reticence to buy the unknown wine. To steal from Wickes and give to Tesco: "It's got our name on it. Finest*".

This development has enlarged the repertoire available on the shelves. Fiano, a white grape variety from Italy, is a good example of a wine that barely existed in the UK a few years ago outside of specialist wine shops and is now quite widely available. Pecorino and Grechetto may well go the same way.

Own-label has another important commercial advantage to a supermarket. Because they own the label they can choose which supplier should fill their bottles. For example, if the supplier of an own-label Australian Shiraz fails to provide the right service, quality or price the supermarket can switch to another, usually without consumers noticing or indeed caring. To us the wine remains the same.

There are only a few big supermarkets and there are a lot of wine suppliers wanting to sell big volumes. It's a buyer's market. This allows the super-markets to negotiate hard to get the best quality for the lowest price. It's a part of the market that is not for the faint hearted, but for suppliers who are commercially strong enough the sales are large. And consumers get good value for money.

So what's not to like? The most common criticism is that supermarket own-label wines have a standardised flavour and lack the individuality of small scale independent producers. Another is that far from producing great value for money, their drive for low price leads to low quality.

These accusations can sometimes be true. But in general they hold their own against – or beat – other wines of the same price and origin. Rather than being a criticism, a standardised flavour is a good thing if it means that the next bottle will taste the same as the last one. Some variety and difference are found in top end own-label ranges. And many producers who have their own brands also fill supermarket own-label bottles, blurring the difference between them.

Ironically "It's got our name on it" is the supermarket's biggest problem as well as their biggest asset. Supermarket own-label wines do not have a prestigious image. You probably wouldn't take one on a first date. If you want to impress someone or make a statement you'd more likely buy an independent label because it feels better, even if it isn't.

M&S, Sainsbury and Waitrose all have some excellent own label Champagnes. I am a big fan of Tesco's Premier Cru. But I keep it hidden in the fridge and wrap the bottle under a kitchen towel when serving it to guests. They always say how nice it is, but I wonder if they would say the same if they saw the label first. I hesitate to give it as a gift or take it to a party. Perhaps I should have the courage of my convictions. But there is always the worry about what other people will think.

IN ONE GULP

Overall own-label wines are of a good standard. "It's got our name on it" is a powerful motivation for supermarkets to seek out quality and value.

Should I trust the medals on wine bottles?

When people are asked what influences their decision about which wine to buy, medals and awards come towards the bottom of the list. They are way below price, country of origin, grape type, promotional offer, and a friend's recommendation.

It is right to pay little attention to medals and awards. As with the Oscars for film and the Man Booker prize for fiction, they are not an objective statement of what is best, nor are they a guarantee that you will like the wine.

Wine-tasting competitions are necessarily partial. They have different rules and formats for tasting. They cannot help being influenced by the culture of the country they take place in and the style of wines most popular there, or the country that the judges come from. A wine winning a gold medal at a tasting competition in California may not appeal at all to drinkers in Bordeaux, whose idea of what a good wine tastes like is very different.

The sheer numbers are daunting. If each of the estimated 50,000 wineries in the world produces an average of 10 wines, it means there are hundreds of thousands in existence. Only a tiny number are entered into competitions. Some competitions are open to any wine, while others are restricted to a specific country, region or grape variety. Either way, even the most ambitious tasting competitions feature just a tiny minority of wines produced in the world.

Wine tasting competitions are subjective. On a certain day a limited group of wines is assessed under the rules of a particular competition by a few judges whose ability, preferences, prejudices and focus on the task are unknown to us. Without personal knowledge of these points, why would anyone have faith in the results?

In an effort to preserve neutrality the wines are usually tasted 'blind' without the judges knowing what they are. They are tasted one after the other in huge numbers and without food. They are not drunk but spat out. This is not how normal people experience wine.

Judging wine in this way is a problem because our interpretation of it is very context-specific. A professional taster's appreciation of a wine on a cold February morning in a bleak London tasting room is likely to differ from that of a group of friends drinking it on a balmy summer evening at a riverside restaurant in York. How much we like a wine depends as much on us, and everything around us, as on what is inside the bottle.

Perhaps aggregating competition results might be useful. If a wine won time after time in many different competitions – like tennis champions Federer, Nadal or Djokovic – it would have a strong claim to being a world beater. It would also show there is consistency in the way people judge.

But studies show that the results are inconsistent. A wine that wins a gold medal in one competition may win nothing in another. Similarly, when two bottles of the same wine are entered in a competition, one of the bottles can win gold, while the other wins nothing. Judges may award different scores to the same wine on different days. Some wines take time to 'open up' their smell and flavour and receive different scores when tasted 10 minutes or three hours after opening.

With so many variables in wine tasting it is not surprising that a study of 13 wine competitions by The Journal of Wine Economics in the USA concluded that "the likelihood of receiving a Gold medal can be statistically explained by chance alone."

In some parts of the world, especially the USA and Asia, the reputation of some judges has a big impact on sales. When they say a wine is excellent its sales take off. Wineries and retailers are keen to maximise the benefit and actively publicise the results. A judge who gives a lot of high scores is likely to get more publicity for him or herself. Whether conscious or not, there is a danger that wines could be over rated as a result.

The elephant in the room is personal taste. Even if there was a wine that became the Roger Federer of its era, winning time after time in blind tastings around the world, there's no guarantee you or I would like it.

Medals are not the route to finding a wine you will like. Just as for film, theatre or music, it's much better to trust the recommendation of a friend or reviewer whose taste you agree with.

If you find yourself in front of the forest of bottles on the shelf with no idea what to buy, try to recall a wine you liked before and look for a similar type. Read the back label and shelf information, talk to the staff (if there are any) or use one of the specialist mobile apps to identify a wine and its taste. It's always better to experiment with considered intent than to let the marketing medal or promotional discount do the thinking for you.

IN ONE GULP

Don't rely on medals to find a wine you will like the taste of. It's better to follow recommendations from people whose taste you trust. Wine tasting competitions are too subjective and partial to be a reliable guide.

What is the best wine?

This is what everyone wants to know. It's the question that gets asked more than any other.

Is it the wine… that costs the most?

that sells the most bottles?

that is most widely distributed?

that has most articles written about it?

that wins most often in tasting competitions?

that features most in the world's best restaurants?

that super taster American Robert Parker rates most highly?

None of these is the answer.

High price may be due to age, scarcity or a host of reasons other than taste. A wine may sell the most in one country, but very little in another. It may be sold widely for a few years, then disappear altogether. Tasting competitions are limited to the wines entered and are as fallible and inconsistent as the human beings who judge them. Media articles are designed to attract readers. Great restaurants aim to please a particular clientele. Super tasters' views are culturally specific and often disagreed with.

There isn't a timeless, objectively best wine any more than there is a best film, food or piece of music. The interpretation of what is best is found inside us, not the bottle. We each have our own tastes and preferences. My best and your best are not the same. And thank goodness for that.

There are really only two types of wine – those you like and those you don't.

The one you like most may change with time, place and occasion. If we have a favourite it must surely be the one we want to drink regardless of circumstance.

If you were marooned on a desert island and could have just one wine with you for the rest of your days, what would it be? The answer is your best wine.

On condition there was a solar powered fridge or cold stream on the island, mine would be a sparkling wine, if possible Champagne, and preferably the brand I was most enjoying at the time of the shipwreck. It would be a fizz I had drunk at a special time with friends. I would sip away my days under the palm tree reliving the memories.

Age matters too when it comes to best. Not the age of the drink but the age of the drinker. A male friend who has earned his stripes in the drinking game described the evolution of his preferences like this:

"At twenty I went for rum and coke or sweet cider. When I hit thirty I was drinking beer with my mates and white wine at home. By forty I liked strong red wines. Around fifty I was drinking red and white wines of average strength. Now I'm over sixty I prefer lighter reds."

So the best drink depends on your stage of life when the shipwreck happens. How terrible to be marooned with a sweet cider at forty or a strong red wine at twenty.

The more you experiment with different grapes, regions and countries, the more exposure you have to different flavours. Noting the ones you like most, and what it is about them that appeals to you, is the only true way to discover what you like best. There is no real short cut, except perhaps following the recommendation of a friend whose tastes align with yours. But it's a lot more fun to do it yourself.

Right now my best wine is the one I am going to drink next.

IN ONE GULP

There is no such thing as a universally best wine, only what we personally like most. If you were marooned on a desert island and could drink just one wine for the rest of your days what would it be? The answer is your best wine.

Is red wine good for health?

There was a time not so very long ago when wine was sold in Chemist shops. Imagine it: "Packet of Paracetamol and a bottle of Aussie Shiraz please". Today all the talk is about how bad alcohol can be and the dangers of excessive drinking. So where did the idea that red wine has health-giving properties come from?

It all started twenty years ago when the American TV show 60 minutes broadcast a programme about the 'French Paradox'. A scientist at Bordeaux University discovered that the French have a relatively low rate of coronary heart disease despite devouring their way through mountains of Brie, croissants and other foods high in saturated fats. He suggested the red wine they drank might have a counterbalancing effect to their cholesterol enhancing diet.

The Americans loved the idea that the beneficial qualities in the vin rouge allowed the French to eat rich foods without dying young. Red wine quickly gained an image as a 'healthy product' and sales soared. The French were delighted. Their Bordeaux region is home to the world's most highly reputed expensive red wines, and France's enormous annual wine production is one of the largest in the world. The paradox was good for business.

But was it true?

That was back in the early 1990s. Many scientific studies since have explored the question without any conclusive evidence of what we want to hear: drinking red wine is good for health.

Even today the debate swings back and forth. Every month there seems to be a new story saying it is, or it isn't, or it may be depending on who you are. Like this one from the Mail Online:

RED WINE CAN BE GOOD FOR YOU – BUT ONLY IF YOU ARE NOT ALREADY HEALTHY

Resveratrol is found in the skins of red grapes and a glass of red wine a day has been put forward as the reason for the longevity of the French, despite a fat rich diet.

But a study of healthy post-menopausal women found those given an over-the-counter resveratrol supplement were no healthier than others who took a dummy pill.

They gave the 15 women 75mg of resveratrol daily, the same amount they would get from drinking eight litres of red wine, and compared their insulin sensitivity to 14 others who received a placebo..... (the) data demonstrate it does not have metabolic benefits in relatively healthy, middle-aged women.

EIGHT LITRES of wine a day! You'd never wake up again if you got your dose of resveratrol by drinking it, which seems a high price to pay for something that was shown to be ineffective.

Just a few weeks earlier the Mail reported a different angle on red wine's benefits:

RED WINE IS GOOD FOR CUTTING BLOOD PRESSURE (BUT YOU NEED TO TAKE OUT THE ALCOHOL)

A study shows for the first time that natural antioxidant compounds in red wine – not the alcohol – are good for your heart health. Researchers in Spain say the alcohol weakens the ability of red wine to cut blood pressure, effectively cancelling out any benefits. They found that men at high risk for heart disease had lower blood pressure after drinking non-alcoholic red wine every day for four weeks.

The Spanish researchers are quoted as saying "Consumption of de-alcoholised red wine might be useful in preventing low to moderate degree hypertension".

So it's not wine, it's more like grape juice and it might be useful, which means it also might not, and the test was made with high risk people, so we are no wiser for those with average risk. What they seem to be saying is forget the wine, just go for the antioxidants.

It's clearly not an easy subject. Drinks Business, a serious publication in the drinks industry, reported a study which on first reading seems like a joke. Under the heading **RED WINE IMPROVES HEART HEALTH IN PIGS** they reported:

"Pigs that drink red wine have better blood flow to the heart than those that drink vodka, a new study has found."

In fact it turns out that red wine was mixed in the food of some pigs and vodka in the food of others. The report continued:

The study, conducted by Frank Sellke M.D, chief of cardiothoracic surgery at Rhode Island Hospital, looked into the effects of red wine and vodka on pigs with high cholesterol.

"There has been previous research touting the benefits of moderate consumption of wine, but we wanted to test the effects of both wine and vodka in conjunction with high cholesterol," Sellke said. "What we found is that moderate consumption of both alcohols may reduce cardiovascular risk, but that red wine may offer increased protection due to its antioxidant properties....

Both red wine and vodka may assist in preventing hardening of the arteries and other cardiac issues... Whether these beneficial effects will be mirrored in humans remains to be seen."

With so many "mays" the case is far from proven – for pigs let alone humans.

A third article in the Mail seemed to kill off any lingering hopes of drinking or munching our way to health:

CHOCOLATES AND RED WINE MAY NOT BE SO GOOD FOR YOU AS SCIENTISTS SAY THERE IS NO EVIDENCE THEY BATTLE HEART DISEASE

But an article in The Telegraph threw out a lifeline, if not for health, at least for dieting. This time it wasn't pigs but bees:

RED WINE 'COULD HELP YOU LOSE WEIGHT'

Drinking red wine could help you lose weight by suppressing your appetite and preventing you from overeating, a study suggests. Researchers found that when bees were fed resveratrol, a compound found in red wine, they ate less food afterwards. While bees normally gorge themselves on sugary foods when they are freely available, those which had been fed resveratrol chose to stop eating once they had taken on enough to meet their energy needs.

But we aren't bees, and we don't gorge all the time unless stopped by a glass or two of red wine. Far from eating less when they drink red wine, many people eat more. Their consumption of crisps, peanuts and other foods increases dramatically and is often followed by wolfing down as many chocolate bars and packets of Haribo as they can lay their hands on. Add in the fact that wine itself contains quite a lot of calories and the idea that drinking it will help weight loss is unconvincing to say the least.

The belief in red wine as beneficial to health is perhaps most widespread in China. The colour red symbolises good fortune and joy, and the majority of grape wine drunk by the Chinese is red. A Chinese wine producer told me it is common for women to dab red wine on their faces before retiring for the night in the belief it is good for the skin.

Within Europe the Wine Information Council acts as a focal point for scientists and research centres dealing with issues of health, and the social and cultural aspects of wine drinking. They believe that moderate drinking of up to two 125ml glasses of red wine a day is beneficial (a bit less for women, a bit more for men).

According to the Council, aggregated information from many studies shows that moderate drinkers live longer on average than both heavy drinkers and those who abstain, especially when looking at men over 40 and post-menopausal women. They favour drinking wine with food rather than on its own and are careful to warn against exceeding the moderate limits.

However a report from Gothenburg University says that moderate drinking only has a strong protective effect in 15% of the population. These people carry a gene that appears to significantly reduce the risk of coronary heart disease when combined with alcohol. For the rest there is no benefit.

The claims and counter claims continue. Twenty years after the French paradox the jury is still out.

There is no '2 a day' for glasses of red wine as there is '5 a day' (400gms) for fruit and veg as recommended by the World Health Organisation. The '5 a day' contribute nutrients we need for a healthy body, and work against serious health problems such as heart disease, strokes, type 2 diabetes and obesity. Some of the compounds found in red wine might be beneficial in isolation, but they are also found in other things, and the quantities needed make wine a dangerous delivery system. Resveratrol, for example, is more safely bought in tablet form as a health supplement.

If the physical health benefits of wine are dubious, its role as one of life's great pleasures is not. Wine enhances social occasions and contributes to our sense of wellbeing. Perhaps it is this, the happiness it brings, that helps the French to live a little longer. It's certainly reason enough to drink it.

But we should keep an eye on how much we drink. James Bond quantities should be avoided. According to a study of Ian Fleming's 14 Bond novels published in the British Medical Journal, James's consumption amounted to 92 units a week, over 6.5 times the recommended maximum. This would have left him incapable of killing international terrorists and seducing beautiful women, and almost guaranteed him serious liver disease.

The UK Government's recommended maximum alcohol consumption for James and the rest of us is 14 units a week. These should be spread over several days, with no binge drinking and some days without alcohol. Following this advice means drinking no more than 2-3 units a day, or about one 175ml medium glass of 13% wine.

Units vary with the amount of alcohol in a drink - the more alcohol it has the more units it contains. A typical wine at 12% alcohol has:

9 units per 75cl bottle

3 units per 250cl large glass

2.1 units per 175ml medium glass

1.5 units per 125ml small glass

IN ONE GULP

Wine in moderation enhances life and friendship. Making us physically healthy is not its job. Many scientific studies have looked at specific potential health benefits with varying outcomes. As yet there is no definitive answer.

Is it true that organic wine doesn't give you a headache?

For most of us drinking vast amounts of booze produces a thumping hangover, headache included. It doesn't matter if the three bottles of red Corbières were organic, bio-dynamic or made on the moon, too much alcohol leaves you feeling wretched. Sometimes you hate yourself so much that you promise never to drink again. And this time you really mean it.

But some people suffer headaches when they drink even a small amount. This is not due to excess alcohol but a reaction to something in the wine. If nasty chemicals are the cause, could organic wines be the way to headache free drinking?

The key difference between organic and conventional wines is how the vines are treated in the vineyard. Organic grapes are grown without the use of synthetic chemical insecticides, pesticides or fertilisers. You can usually tell if a vineyard is organic because it is full of life. Insects, birds and plants thrive in the natural environment. In contrast, chemically treated vineyards are often beautifully neat and tidy but as silent as the night, the vines lined up like rows of soldiers sleeping on parade.

The second difference is in the winemaking – the processes used to turn the grapes into wine and keep it fresh. The chemical sulphur dioxide is added to inhibit things the winemaker doesn't want. It is used to stop bad bacteria developing and as a preservative to prevent the wine ending up like vinegar. It smells like a recently struck match, and you may catch a whiff of it in wines with a high dosage. Organic wines are obliged to use less sulphur than 'normal' wines.

Sulphur dioxide was thought to be a potential cause of headaches. As organic wine contains less, sufferers hoped it might be the answer. However research has shown that while sulphur can provoke allergic and asthmatic reactions, it does not cause headaches. There is a lot more sulphur in dried fruits than in wine, and nobody complains of a stonking headache after eating a handful of dried apricots.

Similarly, most people who complain of getting a headache from wine associate it with reds. But red wines have less sulphur than whites, so if sulphur were to blame it should be white wines that were more associated with headaches.

Another possibility is that the chemical insecticides, pesticides and fertilisers used in the vineyard are transported by the grapes into the wine we drink, causing headaches and other problems. Organic wine has to be made without using these chemicals.

The idea of gulping down a load of synthetic chemicals every time we enjoy a glass of wine is hardly appealing, headaches or not. After all, pesticides and insecticides are designed to kill something. Organic is better for the environment and our health. But as yet there is no evidence the chemical products used in conventional vineyards end up in our stomachs in a dangerous quantity.

Research suggests that a naturally occurring substance called tyramine could be the cause of headaches. It is found in cured and fermented foods such as aged cheese and salami, and is plentiful in red wine. Consume lots of those together and you might be reaching for the paracetamol.

But all we know for sure is that different people react differently. Some characteristics that are poison to one are insignificant to another. If very oaky, tannic or rough tasting red wines feel to you like a headache waiting to happen, stay away from them.

My cousin Tom avoided red wine because it gave him a headache. I didn't know this and opened a bottle of organic Côtes du Rhône for us to share. Wondering if organic might be the answer to his problem, Tom gave it a try. The next morning he was as right as rain. Was it the placebo effect, a lower level of tyramine, or because it was a high quality natural product? Perhaps it doesn't really matter so long as it worked.

Drinking wine is pleasurable, feeling lousy afterwards isn't. **Here is an anti-headache and anti-hangover strategy.** The more of it you follow the better you should feel:

Drink after eating

Don't drink more than a couple of small glasses a day (250 ml, a third of a bottle)

Drink slowly. Give your liver a chance to process the alcohol before it hurts.

Drink an equal amount of water. Or add some to the wine

Drink lower alcohol wine. Rather than 14% or 15% aim for 12% or less

Ditch the sugar. That's sweet wines as well as chocolate. Sugar and alcohol combined increases headache risk

Dabble with organic and bio-dynamic, it might work for you

Drink more water

Drink more water

Drink more water

IN ONE GULP

Organic wine won't prevent you getting a hangover from excessive drinking. The alcohol will do its worst whatever conditions the grapes are grown in. Some people who suffer headaches from drinking even small amounts say they get them less, or not at all, with organic wines. It varies from one person to another.

Which wines have the fewest calories?

The bad news is that alcohol has a lot of calories. It has almost twice as many calories as sugar and only slightly fewer than fat. The good news is that it's easy to steer away from high calorie wines towards skinnier versions. Wine has calories because of the alcohol and sugar. The more it has of each the higher the calorie content.

When grapes are fermented to make wine their sugar turns into alcohol. The more sugar there is in the grapes the more alcoholic the wine can become. Any natural sugar left unfermented, plus any more the winemaker adds, determines how sweet the wine is.

Drinking a big glass of wine with high alcohol and high sweetness gives you calorie max. A small glass with lower alcohol and less sweetness keeps the calories down.

A small glass is 125ml, medium 175ml and large 250ml. 250ml is a third of a bottle, so three large glasses in an evening and you have downed the lot. A typical 13% alcohol bottle contains around 600 calories – just under a third of the average daily amount required by a woman and a quarter for a man. Two medium size glasses have about the same calories as a burger or chicken tikka. If counting the calories is your priority then enemy number one is drinking a lot. Enemy number two is the amount of alcohol in your wine and number three is the sugar.

Grapes grown in hot climates develop more natural sugar. As a result they have the potential to be more alcoholic and thus more calorific. Hot wine producing areas like Australia, California and the south of France (e.g. Châteauneuf-du-Pape) often have wines with 13-15% alcohol. Colder areas like Germany (Riesling), northern Italy (Soave) or the north of France (Muscadet, Sancerre) are usually 10-13%.

European wines tend to have lower alcohol than those from the southern hemisphere, and white wines less than red. Where the sun shines long and hard the calories grow.

Today there are two types of wine catering specifically for the 'light' market. Low alcohol wines at 5.5% are made by removing some of the alcohol after the full strength wine has been made. They are 5.5% because the alcohol duty is less at this level so they can be sold at lower prices. At 45-60 calories for a 125ml glass they are well below a normal wine at around 100. Blossom Hill and Gallo from California, First Cape from South Africa, and Banrock Station from Australia are amongst the bigger names including 5.5% wines in their portfolio. The problem with this type of wine is that removing alcohol also removes flavour. They are not to everyone's taste.

The other 'light' wines are made from grapes that have less sugar in them and are naturally lower in alcohol. Some New Zealand producers are making 9% Sauvignon Blanc and Riesling wines, Jacobs Creek from Australia have a 10.5% Sauvignon Blanc, and the slightly spritzy Vino Verde from Portugal is between 8.5%-11.0%.

The longest established player in the low calorie wine game is that champion of the waistline Weight Watchers. They may not be the first name that springs to mind in connection with wine but they have been successfully trumpeting a range of lower alcohol, lower calorie wines since 2002. These include a White and a Rosé at 8.5% from Germany, both with 75 calories per 125ml glass. Least calorific of all are wines with no, or virtually no, alcohol. Also made by removing the alcohol from normal wines, they do not have a great track record for their taste. But as technology progresses things are looking up. Natureo from Torres, one of Spain's great wine producers, has 0.5% alcohol and 24 calories per 125ml glass. For flavour and taste it leads the pack by a country mile.

If you are tempted to manage your calorie intake by cutting down on bread, pasta or buckwheat to leave room for calories from wine, please don't. For a start the alcohol is not good for your liver. On top of which the calories in alcohol are 'empty', meaning they have no nutritional value, so they can't replace those in food. To cap it all alcohol gives you the munchies and you might end up eating crisps, chips and other calorie-laden monsters.

Six words are the key to cutting calories from wine: drink lower, drink drier, drink less.

IN ONE GULP

The calories in wine come mostly from the alcohol, secondly from the sugar. The lower the alcohol the fewer the calories. To reduce calories choose lower alcohol, drier wines, and drink less.

Why shouldn't I drink red wine with fish?

A friend who loves his hunting and fishing joked that matching wine with food is easy: White wine with fish, red wine with meat, no wine for vegetarians. He is wrong, and not only for the veggies.

The principle of matching food and wine is that they should combine well together. Critically, neither should overpower the other. Nor should the combination make one taste weird, nor produce an unpleasant new third flavour. The key is to find a balance of complementary flavours. This could be because they are similar, or because they are contrasting.

Traditional thinking was that as white wines are lighter and less overpowering than reds, they are a better match for the soft, light flavour and texture of fish. People living in regions with both vineyards and fishing industries traditionally match dry whites with the harvest from the sea. Muscadet around Nantes in northern France, Picpoul de Pinet near Sète in the south, and Albariño from Galicia in northwest Spain are good examples. But it's not as simple as that.

Some fish, such as tuna and swordfish, have strong almost meaty flavours. Others like cod have much lighter flavours. Just as importantly the texture is quite different, one dense the other soft and flaky. Such big differences suggest different wine styles to partner them.

Beyond these natural contrasts, the flavour of the fish can be transformed by the way it is cooked. Pan grilled with spices and garlic or lightly steamed on its own? Barbecued over charcoal or curried? Served with a vibrant salsa verde sauce or alone? The method of cooking can dramatically alter the flavour, and so your decision about the wine to go with it.

When you know the nature of the fish and how it is cooked you can choose a wine. Could be red, white, or rosé. It depends on the flavours and style of a particular wine, not its colour. A heavily oaked, strongly flavoured white wine will drown a light fish dish, whereas a lighter fruity red won't. The powerful flavours of those swordfish steaks will swallow up a meagre Pinot Grigio but meet their match in a robust red Rioja.

The days of the "white wine with fish, red wine with meat" straitjacket are gone. Think of the texture and strength of flavours in the food, whether you want a wine that is similar or contrasting, and then choose a style and colour. Anything that works for you is good. There is no right and wrong.

If you are in doubt about which wine to choose go for one you like, even if you are not sure how well it will pair with the fish (or the meat, or the vegetarian dish). If you like the wine and the food independently of each other, you will enjoy the meal. But if you don't like the wine, it doesn't matter how often you are told it is a good match for the food, you won't enjoy the meal as much.

As a guide to matching food and wine, pair lighter flavoured wines with lighter flavoured dishes, medium with medium and strong with strong. Try chilling light and medium reds in the fridge, especially if the weather and environment are warm. And remember that your taste is affected by what is outside the bottle as well as what is inside. Match the wine with the ambience and mood as well as the food.

IN ONE GULP

There should be no colour bars when matching food and wine. Complementary flavours and personal preference are what matter. Red wines are often great with strongly flavoured fish and those which are cooked with added flavours.

Why doesn't the wine I brought back from holiday taste as good at home?

People sometimes talk about wine 'not travelling well'. But it's usually not the wine, it's us. The delicious wine you drank on holiday tastes different because you are not on holiday.

Wine in a bottle won't change much unless it's exposed to hostile conditions. Put a bottle of Pinot Grigio on the back shelf of the car when you drive back from Italy in mid-August and it should be nicely cooked by the time you arrive home. Especially if it is in a clear glass bottle rather than the more protective green or brown. Excessive heat and sunlight will alter the flavour, but otherwise the wine will be the same at home as it was out there.

But we are not the same. A recurring theme in these pages is that we 'taste' with all our senses, not just our taste buds. What we see, hear, touch, smell and of course taste combine to affect our interpretation of wine. Even the most basic plonk can taste great after tanning in the sun and frolicking in the waves, the cares of the world and thoughts of the office a million miles away. The sound of the music playing, the dry taste of the heat, the feel of the sand, the smell of the pine trees – all of these are missing when you drink the wine at home on a cold grey February evening. No wonder it doesn't taste the same.

There is a growing realisation of how important context is to our taste perception, and not only for wine. Trials show how changes in light, colour and music affect people's perception of the same wine. A study reported in the Research Digest of the British Journal of Psychology shows that people drinking the same wines described them differently according to the music they were listening to at the time. When asked if they thought the wine was powerful and heavy, subtle and refined, mellow and soft, or zingy and refreshing they "tended to think their wine had the qualities of the music they were listening to."

A German study found that people tasted wine 50% sweeter when drunk under red light than under blue or white. In a UK test winemaker Roberto Vicente of Spanish brand Campo Viejo tasted his own wine under different coloured lighting. He found it tasted as he expected under white light, sweeter and less bitter under red, and unrecognisable under green.

Professor Charles Spence of Oxford University who carried out the study was reported by the Daily Telegraph as saying:

"I believe the results of our study will extend to restaurants and bars reconsidering the colour of tablecloths, glassware, cutlery and even the colour of pictures on the walls".

Environment, context and mood all affect how we taste. The best way to relive the taste of that holiday wine is to take the same holiday next year. Failing that try recreating the environment as much as you can – choose a hot day, invite the friends you were on holiday with to come round, cook the same food, play the same music, look at the photos. Or just pour yourself a decent glass, close your eyes and let your imagination do the rest.

IN ONE GULP

How we perceive taste is about what is going on outside the bottle as well as inside. When we drink wine brought back from a holiday the wine is the same but the holiday is missing. That's what makes the wine taste different.

Does it matter
what Kind of glass
I drink wine out
of ?

My first collection of glasses came from the local petrol station. In those days they gave out vouchers for every gallon you bought. When you had amassed enough you got a free glass or two. They were a mixture of tumblers and wine glasses of different shapes and sizes. This rag bag collection held my first wines. I have never looked back.

Why should the glass matter? Or whether it's made of glass rather than plastic or paper?

The most obvious reason is style. If you are putting on a classy show you want everything to be perfect. You don't want a special dinner in a smart restaurant on your mum's birthday to be spoilt because the glasses are the size of acorns and ugly as hell. They need to look good because it's a special occasion and you want to impress.

But a classy glass does more than add to the ambience of the occasion. It also suggests that the wine inside will be good.

Because what we see sets our expectation of what is to come, we really might like the taste of the wine more if the glass is stylish and appealing.

But does the specific shape of the glass matter?

Austrian Claus Riedel thought so. A ninth generation glass maker, he spent years studying how glass shapes match the flavours and aromas of different wines. In 1958 he released the wrist defying 'Sommeliers Burgundy Grand Cru' glass which holds a bottle and a half of wine and is now part of a collection in the Museum of Modern Art in New York. Inspired by the Bauhaus design principle that "form follows function", Riedel glasses have gone on to become the gold standard in the industry.

Today Riedel supply a bewildering array of glasses that are both elegant and functional. Believing that the experience of drinking each type of wine can be improved by having a glass to match, they offer specific glasses for everything from Sauvignon Blanc to Cabernet Sauvignon, Tempranillo, Pinot Noir, Chardonnay and many, many more.

However not everyone is convinced that the glass shape can really affect the taste. Opinion amongst wine professionals is mixed. Studies carried out in America found no statistically relevant evidence to support the idea.

The theory is that the 'right' kind of glass will enhance the flavours and aromas in a wine. The basic division is between red and white wines. Reds are said to require larger glasses and a wider bowl so the flavours are released by swirling and aeration, while white wine glasses are generally narrower and smaller to keep the wine cold.

Blindfold under neutral conditions everyday wine drinkers are unlikely to experience a significantly different taste from one type of glass to the next. Context and what we see can give the glass importance. But let's not forget three fundamentals:

If the wine is a style you don't like, no amount of glass design wizardry is going to transform it into one that you do. Equally, you won't be put off a wine you like by drinking it from a petrol station tumbler.

Feeling in a good mood, having a great time with mates, glorious weather, being in love, watching a great DVD – these are the kind of things that make wine taste good. The shape of the glass is way down the list. One of the greatest memories I have of drinking wine (and a few other alcoholic drinks) was an evening with three friends sitting on the floor of an Ibis hotel room in Bordeaux joyfully emptying the mini bar. We drank with tumblers from the bathroom and cups from the coffee-making kit.

Most of us drink wine without focusing on the nuances of flavour and aroma in the glass. After sharing a bottle of red one evening I asked my wife what she thought of it. "Oh, I don't know, I didn't notice, I just drank it" she said. Herr Riedel's glasses would be wasted in such a situation.

Whether you simply drink wine or decide to start tasting it by consciously paying attention to the flavours and aromas, these common sense tips are worth following:

- Avoid very small glasses. They are awkward to use and need constant refilling.

- Get ones that are big enough to be no more than half full when they have a decent amount in them. This looks generous and allows a bit of air to mix in and bring out the flavours, depending how quickly you knock it back.

- For whites and chilled reds get glasses with stems long enough to hold, so you don't grab the glass and warm up the wine. But ensure they are short enough to fit in the dishwasher.

- Use glasses that are clean and don't smell of lemon fragrance from the machine.

- Use a flute for Champagne and sparkling wine if seeing the bubbles rise up the length of the glass is part of what makes it special for you.

How much the glass matters depends largely on you. If you like beautifully designed glasses by all means spend money on buying a range of them. They will add class and interest to any occasion. But if you don't have the budget, space or interest then a versatile, dishwasher proof glass such as the Riedel Vinum Chianti or Ouverture Magnum will do very well for both red and white.

IN ONE GULP

The type of glass plays a part in our impression of taste and event. But most people will not taste a difference in the same wine served in different glasses if they have their eyes shut. Company and occasion affect our enjoyment of wine more than the glass.

Why do professional wine tasters slurp and chew wine?

Tasting the full flavours in a wine is very different from just drinking it.

Most people take a gulp and swallow. The wine just surfs over the 3-10,000 taste buds in our mouth, before continuing en route down the throat to the stomach. We taste it, but fleetingly. To taste in greater depth the wine needs to be kept in the mouth for longer, coating the taste buds more fully.

But that's only half the story. The flavours and aromas in wine are shy. They become bolder and more obvious when they meet oxygen in the air. It's the reason people say a wine should 'breathe'. When a taster has sipped but not swallowed, they draw in extra air to give the wine a blast of oxygen. This makes the flavours more pronounced. Moving the wine and air mixture around ensures it gets well mixed and spread across a lot of taste buds.

This process inevitably makes some noise (but can be a lot quieter than the ostentatious performance of some tasters) so you might not want to try it first time in a restaurant. But do try it, because the increase in flavour is noticeable.

Another way to experience the full flavour of a wine is to hold your nose before you take a sip. Once you have the wine in your mouth, with your nose still clamped shut, think about what you can taste. It'll be something but not much. Then still keeping the wine in your mouth, let go of your nose and breathe in through it. Notice the sudden explosion of taste. It's the flavour releasing role of the air again, much like getting your taste back after a heavy cold. Tasting flavours fully means using your nose.

This 'deep tasting' is done by wine producers, buyers and critics for professional reasons. They want to experience the taste to the maximum in order to judge it. But even they drink normally most of the time.

IN ONE GULP

Professional wine-tasters mix wine and air in their mouths. The oxygen interacts with the wine and increases the intensity of flavour. Moving it around their mouth coats more taste buds, so enabling them to experience the taste more fully.

Why do waiters ask us to taste wine before serving it?

One evening in an Edinburgh restaurant I was sitting at a table next to a young couple. The guy was trying to look cool and quickly took charge of the wine list. He made his choice and ordered. The waiter returned with the bottle and asked him to taste it. He did so, winced a bit, said it was no good, and asked to see the wine list again. The second bottle he chose didn't meet his approval either, so he sent it back and chose a third. It took four different wines before he was happy. By this time his companion had disappeared to talk to friends at another table.

When I finished my meal I headed for the waiter and asked him why he had agreed to change so many bottles. He said it was company policy to ensure that customers were always happy with their wine. I asked him if this included their simply not liking the taste, even if there was nothing wrong with the wine. He said it did.

The not-so-cool guy in Edinburgh had struck lucky. In most restaurants a taste is offered to check if the wine is faulty, not to ask whether you like it. Faulty almost always means corked. As discussed in the chapter 'what is a corked wine?', this means spotting the musty, wet cardboard flavour that they have.

Some of the wines the guy in Edinburgh rejected had screw caps not corks. Wines with screw caps can't be ruined by an infected cork because they don't have one. They don't really need tasting before serving. Once in a while the TCA that can infect a cork spreads throughout the winery, in which case even a wine with a screwcap might suffer, but this is so rare as to be insignificant.

The ritual of checking a wine at table originated long ago, when most restaurant wines came from a specific property and vintage. Before pouring a taste the waiter would present the unopened bottle for inspection. If the property or year on the label was not the one ordered it need not be accepted.

Once visually approved, the waiter would then open the bottle and present the cork for inspection. A crumbling or sodden cork could be a sign that it had lost its ability to prevent the air from ruining the wine. But the main purpose was to check that the cork had the name of the Chateau printed on it. If it didn't, the suspicion was that the original wine had been replaced by something cheaper and re-corked. Worse, if the waiter arrived at table with the bottle already open and the cork nowhere to be seen, anything might have been poured into the bottle at the back of the restaurant.

Once the bottle was opened the man – it was of course usually a man – would taste. If he had tasted the same wine before he could recall what it was like and approve or decline. The role of taster may also have been a sign of status and power, showing that the person had authority to approve the wine on behalf of everyone else around the table. In earlier times the opposite may have applied, the lowly food and drink taster risking their own life to protect their master from potential poisoning.

Wine in restaurants is expensive. It's always worth checking that the waiter brings the bottle unopened, that the label matches what you ordered from the wine list, and that you taste to check it's not corked – if it has one.

IN ONE GULP

Waiters offer a taste so you can check that the wine isn't faulty or 'off'. It is not to ask whether you like it.

What is the best way to choose wine in a restaurant?

According to a report by French Wines with Style, only 12% of us feel confident about choosing the right wine in a restaurant. This is hardly surprising. Very few restaurants make it easy or fun. But there are a number of things you can do about this.

The first is to understand the occasion.

Is this a really important meal where everything needs to be perfect, including the wine? If so that means stress, and de-stressing requires planning. It's a time to play safe and avoid mistakes.

Or is it an informal social event where anything goes? Feeling carefree opens the door to choosing wine without anxiety. It's an opportunity to experiment with wines you have never tasted before. Friends and family will still love you if the wine isn't great, and they will love you a little bit more if it is.

For both types of occasion your options depend on the nature of the wine list.

A fine dining place might have a wine list the size of a Harry Potter novel. A long list suggests the restaurant has spent time and money on its wines, so the overall standard should be high and the choice diverse. If they are thinking about their customers, there will be a short wine selection at the front for those who don't want to plough through the whole thing. If they aim to be known for their wines as well as their food, a specialist wine waiter (also known as a sommelier) will be on hand to provide information and recommendations. Expect the wine storage conditions and stock rotation to be good.

On the other hand the wine list in the local Italian may be just three whites, three reds and a rosé. For many people 'less is more' when it comes to wine lists because a small, focused range is easier to choose from. However if the restaurant is modest the wines probably will be too. In this case it's best to stick to well-known names that turn over quickly and stay fresh. Choose the youngest vintages and be sure to avoid the half bottles of rosé that have been stuck out the back for half a century.

Whether the wine list is a marathon or a sprint, the troublesome question is how to pick wines that go with the food.

One option is not to bother. Some people simply look for a wine style they like, choosing the wine before they know what the food will be. Others reason that it's impossible to match food and wine for a group because of all the different dishes, so there is no point trying. By choosing the food and wine independently each can be enjoyed in its own right. If they happen to enhance each other it's a bonus.

This approach is great for avoiding stress about wine. And without stress the evening will be more enjoyable.

But let's assume the job of choosing the wine has unexpectedly fallen into your lap. You decide you will try and match the food and wine for a group. So you need to know:

Is their preference for red, white or rosé?

What style of wine do they like – heavy or light, drier or sweeter, fruity or crisp?

Do they feel like being adventurous and choosing an unknown wine, or playing safe with a type they have had before?

What is the price limit? What are they eating?

How many bottles do you think will be needed? The average is one bottle between three people. You might want to order different wines at the same time to cater for different tastes. Or you might want to plan a few different bottles one after the other to match different courses, or just for the fun of experimenting.

This information is the basis to work from. If you are lucky the wine list will show the wines by style – light, medium and so on – with useful descriptions in understandable English. They may even suggest which wines go well with which dishes.

If the list doesn't enable you to choose with knowledge, use the waiter. The French Wines with Style Report found that only 20% of us say we would ask for help. Perhaps this is because we don't want to look stupid, or perhaps it's because we don't expect the waiters to know anything about wine. Many don't, but it's worth asking them. The good ones who don't know will get someone who does.

Give the waiter all the information you have gathered – the price bracket, your preference for colour and style, what food people are eating, and whether you want to play safe or experiment. These are their tools. If you feel sheepish about shouting out the price limit, point to it on the wine list.

Bear in mind that restaurant prices are usually three or four times the price of an equivalent wine in a shop. An £18 bottle in a restaurant would usually be £5-£6 in a shop, a £30 bottle £8-£10. A few restaurants add the same cash margin to every wine, which makes the more expensive wines relatively cheaper than they would normally be.

Once you have narrowed down the possibilities you may still be unsure what to choose because you haven't drunk any of these exact wines before. Ask if you can taste before buying. If the wine is sold by the glass they will have it open and should agree without question. If you choose without tasting and have followed the waiter's recommendation for a particular bottle only find you don't like it, ask them to change it. A bad recommendation is really the only time you should reject a wine because you don't like the taste, rather than because it is faulty.

If you are in a group of people with different tastes, or if you feel like trying a few different wines, why not buy by the glass? So long as you know the size of the glass (125, 175 or 250 ml) you can work out how much more expensive it is than buying a 750ml bottle. It will usually cost more, but often not much, and occasionally less. Years ago as a hard up student I spent an evening in a Lisbon restaurant ordering glass after glass rather than buying a bottle because they had got the calculation the wrong way round.

So what happens if all this fails? The wine list is incomprehensible, the waiters are useless, there is nothing available to taste, and you are on your own with the decision making.

One thing you shouldn't do is chose the wine that the waiter tells you is "our most popular". This could well be code for 'it's the one we make most money on'. Nor should you choose the second most expensive wine on the list. Many people do, because buying the cheapest looks mean. Some restaurants got wind of this and put their best earners in second place, which means it might be the wine they paid the least for.

Option one is not to worry about the food combination and go for a wine you know and like. Tim Hanni, the man who says we are one of four "vinotypes", suggests matching the wine to the diner not the dinner. If for example you like Merlot, especially if you have a preference for one from a particular country such as Chile, look for a Chilean Merlot. It probably won't be the same wine you have enjoyed before, but the style should be similar.

Option two is to match birds of a feather. Choose lighter flavoured wines with lighter flavoured foods, medium with medium, strong with strong.

Option three is to go for wines that have a great chance of tasting good ll the time, to everyone, with everything. My suggestions for these super-versatile crowd pleasers are:

RED
First choice: Pinot Noir from New Zealand or the USA (preferably Washington State or Oregon but also California). Medium bodied, smooth and succulent with ripe flavours

Second choice: Côtes Du Rhône from France. Usually a little more gutsy but by no means heavy.

I haven't included Burgundy in my first choice although it is the spiritual home of the Pinot Noir grape. There is such a wide variety in quality that unless you already know the wine you can easily be expensively disappointed. As a rule Burgundy is a region where the more you pay the better the quality. And boy can you pay more. Pinot Noir from New Zealand and the USA are more consistent, and while they may not hit the heights of Burgundy they won't plunge to the depths. Most are reliably good.

WHITE

First choice: Verdicchio or Fiano from Italy. Combining the flavour of the New World with the elegance of the Old.

Second choice: Albariño from Spain. Slightly crisper but equally crowd pleasing.

These may not be wines most people drink regularly. The default white for many people today is Pinot Grigio, usually from Italy, and while there are some really great flavoursome wines from that grape variety the general style is too non-descript and watery for me. My recommended wines have a lot more flavour but are equally versatile. They are a BMW to Pinot Grigio's Ford Fiesta.

IN ONE GULP

Focus on identifying a wine you will enjoy before worrying about how it matches the food. Decide on your price limit, recall types of wine you have enjoyed before, read the wine list descriptions, get information from the waiter, ask to taste before you buy. To pair wine with food match birds of a feather – lighter wines with lighter foods, medium with medium, strong with strong. For an important event where everything must be perfect, make contact with the restaurant in advance to discuss the food and wine, using their expertise for recommendations.

What to do next

"Anyone who tries to make you believe that he knows all about wines is obviously a fake."

Leon Adams.

Enjoying wine is about three things: feeling confident about what you are doing, finding ones that you like, and drinking them with friends. Nothing more.

The answers in this book are tools to greater enjoyment from wine. Like all tools, they have to be used to produce results. Here are the 10 best ways to use them:

- Ask what you will

- Never, ever be intimidated or embarrassed

- Make safe choices when you need to, experiment like mad when you don't

- Find a way to remember a wine you love. Take a photo, write a note, sing a song

- Explore the people and stories behind the wines

- Be guided by knowledge or emotion, not price

- Share your discoveries with friends

- Grab the wine list in a restaurant. Be the one to choose

- Drink safely at all times. This is the only life with wine available. Make it last

- Smile. Wine is fun

THE AUTHOR

After completing a degree in African Studies at Edinburgh University, Jerry Lockspeiser's first proper job was teaching teenagers to ride motorbikes. He started his first wine business at the age of thirty-two knowing nothing about wine or business. After many years of trial and error he is still learning about both.

Jerry is currently Chairman of Off Piste Wines and writes an opinion column for Harpers Wine & Spirit. The Call My Wine Bluff event he created has raised over a million pounds in support of international development charity ActionAid.

THE MILLIONE FOUNDATION

The revenue the author receives from the sale of this book will be donated to The Millione Foundation, a social business he set up with two wine business friends to fund the building of primary schools in Sierra Leone, West Africa. The schools are built by the local communities in partnership with ActionAid. By 2015 five schools were operational, educating over 1500 children in some of the poorest areas of the country.

The Foundation owns the eponymous Millione wine brand all of whose profits are used to fund the schools.

On drinking the Millione Frizzante Rosé actress Emma Thompson said:

"Oh that's lovely.......full of hope and joy and that's the best taste I've ever tasted in a wine"

www.millionewine.com

THE ILLUSTRATOR

Lotte Beatrix Crawford is an illustrator and Art History lecturer with a BA from Kingston art school and MA from University College London. Her work includes a picture book 'The Christmas Wren' with National Poet of Wales Gillian Clarke for the Dylan Thomas centenary and branding for the Pump St Bakery in Suffolk. She has illustrated for a variety of magazines dedicated to good food and drink. Examples can be seen at www.lottebeatrix.com.

TO FIND OUT MORE OR GET IN CONTACT

Stay in touch through www.yourwinequestions.com or visit www.millionewine.com to learn more about the work of The Millione Foundation in Sierra Leone.

Acknowledgements

Above all I would like to thank the many wine drinkers who felt brave enough to ask me their questions. Without them this book would not exist. Many began with a tentative "I know this may sound stupid but…" I hope they now know that there is nothing stupid about asking these questions.

I would specifically like to thank Dawn Carlisle, Sarah Higson, Beccy Lockspeiser, Deborah Mattinson and Anna Nairn who gave me valuable input on chapters in progress. Rosie Leyden edited them as they evolved, providing essential support when I needed it most. Joe Treasure expertly polished the completed work. Lotte Beatrix's inspiration has provided the wonderful illustrations, Jonas Bergmann Bjornsson and Philippe Griffoul creatively designed the layout. Very significantly, Bjorn Jonasson committed Citizen Press to publishing the book for free to help us build more schools in Sierra Leone. Thank you all so much.